Praise for Robert Vivian's *Least*

"These essays contain some of the finest writing I have ever read. We readers are big mammals. We lumber through life as best we can, leaving so much in our wake unnoticed. Robert Vivian makes up for this short-coming. He's got something extra going on, some reflexive seventh sense, which might be called the ability to make sense of the world. Reading these essays, you grow roots, gain dimension; your universe expands."

SUSAN SALTER REYNOLDS, *Los Angeles Review of Books*

"Vivian's essays are introspective little gems that celebrate and elevate the commonplace. . . . From Michigan to Nebraska to Eastern Europe, an eclectic group of settings provides vivid context for this string of extraordinarily evocative writings. Readers who love the imaginative leaps the mind can make will take pleasure in this unique collection."

MARGARET FLANAGAN, *Booklist*

"Robert Vivian is a rare gift to readers—a writer whose natural subject is the soul. In his essays, whether his setting is Turkey, Hungary, or the hallway of his Michigan home, Vivian invokes and portrays the rich and startling inner realms of experience of which he is both in trembling awe and utterly unafraid."

LAWRENCE SUTIN, author of *When to Go into the Water: A Novel*

"Robert Vivian is one of the finest, most lyrical essayists of his time, giving voice to an internal life fully engaged with a sensuous external world. Vivian writes with illuminating and potent powers about the startling and shimmering wonder all around us. Whether his subject is eating at a Big Boy in Alma, Michigan, or clearing weeds from a Jewish cemetery in Poland, Vivian's prose brings us inside moments of surprising beauty, sadness, heartbreak, love, tenderness, longing, and, most important, hope."

SUE WILLIAM SILVERMAN, author of *Fearless Confessions: A Writer's Guide to Memoir*

"Beautiful essays to read and savor one at a time."

Kirkus Reviews

"With a poet's eye and ear, Vivian elevates the everyday to the universal in a contemplative voice, like 'the least cricket of evening under the porch of a clapboard house, chirping out its one note of everlasting wisdom.'"

BRUCE JACOBS, founding partner, Watermark Books and Café

Praise for Robert Vivian's *Cold Snap as Yearning*

"Crystalline and luminous. . . . The ravishing simplicity of Vivian's prose is perfectly balanced by the peacock-plumed precision of his metaphors, such as the image of crows as the 'dark hangnails of God,' the sound of a broken back as 'the click of a gear lock, or a key turning in a rusty door.'"
Kirkus Reviews

"Each of these vivid essays probes the mystery of encounter, that is, the impermanence of what our five senses tell us, despite the constancy of memory. Each is set in the Midwest, and in each, the author displays his uncanny ability to identify the fading present."
Publishers Weekly

"[Vivian] achieves for his readers a sustained musical pitch on which his memorable observations of the daily and the ordinary can ride."
Georgia Review

"In this collection of personal essays, Robert Vivian offers a series of vivid, intensely reflective, and soul-searching renderings of the lives and landscapes of the Great Plains. . . . The book's many character sketches demonstrate his journalistic eye for detail and poetic ability to pierce the heart. . . . In its most luminescent moments—and there are many in this book—*Cold Snap as Yearning* takes on the pitch and gravity of spiritual autobiography, bringing to mind the work of such writers as Simone Weil and Thomas Merton, though the spiritual realm Vivian evokes is characterized more by divine absence than presence."
Great Plains Quarterly

"Vivian's writing is consistently poetic in the sense that such care has been taken in assembling every sentence, every phrase, that scarcely a word could be changed without lessening the effect. . . . *Cold Snap as Yearning* is a lovely book, a series of sharply focused lessons in introspection, in being on the outside of the world and looking in, only to discover that by looking closely you have magically passed through the mirror and are, to your pleasure, a part of it all."
TED KOOSER, *Lincoln Journal Star*

All I Feel Is Rivers

All
I
Feel
Is
Rivers

Dervish Essays · ROBERT VIVIAN

University of Nebraska Press · Lincoln

Acknowledgments for the use of copyrighted
material appear on pages xi–xii, which
constitute an extension of the copyright page.

Library of Congress
Cataloging-in-Publication Data
Names: Vivian, Robert, 1967– author.
Title: All I feel is rivers:
dervish essays / Robert Vivian.
Other titles: Dervish essays
Description: Lincoln: University of Nebraska
Press, 2020. | Summary: "All I Feel Is Rivers is a
collection of essays in a ground-breaking genre,
the 'dervish essay,' a new kind of hybrid writing
that, though spiritually akin to prose poems,
retains an essayistic form. Vivian's
dervish essays take on grief and loss, the
natural world and climate, spirituality and
ecstasy, all while pushing the boundaries of what
prose can do"—Provided by publisher.
Identifiers: LCCN 2019027687
ISBN 9781496220332 (paperback)
ISBN 9781496221025 (epub)
ISBN 9781496221032 (mobi)
ISBN 9781496221049 (pdf)
Subjects: LCSH: Grief. | Loss (Psychology) |
Nature. | Climate. | Spirituality. | Ecstasy.
Classification: LCC PS3572.I875 A6 2020 |
DDC 814/.54—dc23
LC record available at
https://lccn.loc.gov/2019027687

Set in Arno Pro by Laura Ebbeka.
Designed by L. Auten.

This book is dedicated to T-bird, Aunt Marg of Muskegon, and Yavuz and Semra—harika. And a huge special thanks to Joel Peckham, Jr.—brother from the first day we met.

What do I fear? I am a part of infinity.

EDITH SÖDERGRAN

If only I could leave everything as it is, without moving
a single star or a single cloud. Oh, if only I could!

ANTONIO PORCHIA

I don't believe in the other world. The world is one.
One reality.

ANNA KAMIEŃSKA

CONTENTS

ACKNOWLEDGMENTS

Grateful acknowledgment is made to the following publications, where some of these pieces first appeared:

"Maybe Fall to My Knees." *Belletrist.*

"Yes." *Trampset.*

"O After O." *Breathe Free Press.*

"Dovelike." *December* magazine.

"Pen." *Cargo Literary.*

"To Beg Mercy of a Shadow." *Subprimal.*

"Any Word." *Junto Magazine.*

"Another Kind of Waking." *Flexible Persona.*

"Even Then." *Edify Publications.*

"How Precious Still." *Leaping Clear.*

"All the Rivers of My Days." *Flexible Persona.*

"Other Darks." *Little Leo.*

"Bell." *Belletrist.*

"Essay Transparent Almost to Midnight." *The Offbeat.*

"Bring the River." *Sleet Magazine.*

"Essay as the World's Worst Jeweler." *Red Savina Review.*

"The Waft-Away World." *Two Cities Review.*

"The Woman in Me." *Pithead Chapel.*

"Light Upon Lightly." *Eastern Iowa Review.*

"A Kind of Inner Russia." *Border Crossing.*

"Because There Are Ghosts." *Chautauqua.*

"Come Earthward." *Wraparound South.*

"Essay by the Black Sea." *Small Portions.*

"Gobsmack Essay." *Profane* literary journal.

"Ink of River." *Delmarva Review.*

"Keeper Bees." *Twisted Vine Literary Arts Journal.*

"Letter to Neruda." *Hermeneutic Chaos* literary journal.

"Mother Forever." *Upstreet.*

"Play." *Kindred* magazine.

"Read to You." *Timberline.*

"Some Kind of Holiness." *Stoneboat.*

"Somewhere a Siren." *Guernica.*

"Tell Me Flower." *Kindred* magazine.

"When Water This Earth." *Dirty Chai.*

"God-Husks." *Cherry Tree.*

All I Feel Is Rivers

All I Feel Is Rivers

How Precious Still

Here where the word is beautiful, here where the word is most
true, where I am trembling and silent listening to my own breath-
ing under a harvest moon—here where the backs of my hands
look up at me like burnt fields, where I am poised over the edge
of this page, I ask in wonder and in mercy what night child of sky
will become me in this planet of such tender and ferocious verse,
and who will wander with me down the remaining days of this life
so holy I feel the cool air graze my eyeteeth where the full moon
glows and I wake with happiness to once more be alive this early
hour drenched with mystery in a century that talks too much,
that is too busy and serious except for the trees and animals who
know how to watch and how to listen, loving in all weather and
what moves them to temple stillness where the word is beautiful
and is not even spoken or written, is not even wet with ink but
shining in the dark in great mercy and truth, a beam of light deep
in the night making its way over the valleys and rivers, drawing
clear water up and into itself, saying the one astonishing thing
over and over again, here, where the word is beautiful and naked,
glistening at last with truth and with the aching tenderness of
a whole sky littered with stars whispering like a dying lover on
the doorstep, Oh my love, my precious love, how beautiful it all
is, how wonderful, how precious still, the single tear in my eye
creating a whole lake for you to bathe in, come wade into my
waters, immerse yourself until you are whole.

Even Then

Night, what comes then, soft vowels flowing and I among the grasses to hear them as beginning listener, always a beginning as I lift my head to sounds in the darkness and star chamber, the darkness I hear, the darkness I listen into with all of my breathing, my heart's love so constant it will not stop until I die, and even then, even then, what master crow or bird is to say of it, to breathe and laugh and love of it, night what comes, owl in the dark intent on rabbit as I am on word, maybe meaning, feeling sound, the whole of my early morning life a sacred mystery given over to this rapt listening in the dark, so much listening I cannot get enough of this not knowing, only hearing, hearing what might come or what is already here, so precious still, and all the dictionaries waiting in the lilt-most turning of a page, some kind of onion skin dignity, beckoning almost, reaching out from the depths of oral history, pressing into ink and only one word, one sound enough to save me, a beautiful howl called ache, called yearning, and love as my eyes age precious blue into another sky, night what comes the flora and the fauna and the cold precious breeze as first a word, then another, wild animal of sound and syllable, how you do ache me deep inside the hollow spaces of my bones, one day to roam again and feed another animal, this one earth in precious dawn before dawn, and who taught me to wake and to wonder, was it bobcat, eagle, or deer, why almost everything and the love of moving water, my blood on loan from river, that teaches me how to see through water all the way to paradise, you know the sound, precious songbird and so I say songbird, songbird, can you show me the joy of your two words, bright beads from a never-ending string, oh my brothers and sisters, the holy branches holding and raising up the beauty we cannot bear for seeing/holding/touching your leaves, calling out buds and blossoms in a voice the earth loves as I am grateful-lost among the silences of this cold November morning in the year of the whole world hugging the death knell to her breast until it turns into sunlight just tipping over the horizon, like spilled tea singing a hymn of wire light, and always into the northern gusts of forever sky.

All the Rivers of My Days

Dear echo heard long ago in childhood or before, still I listen faithfully for you each morning, leaning my whole body into the early morning air, my every waking and breathing, dear echo, bare and empty a.m., these scraping words of voice and yearning, dear echo, dear marks on a page imperfect, reaching out to you beneath canyon walls and by the edge of a river and within the river's sweeping depth and current, dear echo and the voices of ancestors speaking so quietly to me I can almost hear them in the inmost rings of trees growing in the dark and slow changing of the seasons as I age, as I wonder about wisdom and the destruction of the world by human hands, dear echo, dear letter, dear poem and strong but tender tone of you that still rings in my bones up into my eyeteeth, humming me anew each day even as I struggle to understand what is required except maybe just this listening, this early morning summons again and again and again, all the rivers of my days and you, dear echo, telling me to look at the stars and moon, to look at my own hands, to say thank you to what is no matter how it comes or in what form, to lift my arms to you, dear echo, dear long ago, to bless the whole sky with my passing and my dying, the miles I still have to walk, the air in my lungs and nostrils, how you are teaching me even now how to say the simplest and most important things, like I love the earth and I love the sound of wind through the trees, the sigh that begins every sentence and the sigh that fades so gently away after the last word is spoken.

Yes

Yes, I dive deeply into words and yes, they somehow hold me
even as they are passing away, and yes to the window and the
doorknob, yes to all the humble implements, pan and dish and
saucer, coffee pot and teaspoon of honey—yes to the beating of
my heart and every heart, yes to the vibrant roundness of every
living creature and the fragrance of lilacs blossoming here in early
June, Yes, I say, and yes again to the spider on a north-facing wall
and yes to the woods beyond and yes to the very word north,
most evocative and mysterious direction on any compass, yes
to the harshness of winter and brief glory of summer and every
rising fish, yes to a bed of pine needles in the forest and yes to
the many peelings of bark that become these utterances—yes
to a piece of paper and yes to this very pen jotting these words
and other words like I love you, like We are out of eggs, like I
have this intense feeling that everything is brief and unspeakably
precious, like The green buds are reaching out to touch my breath,
my tongue, they want me to grow with them—and yes even to
loneliness and to dying, yes to the last time you say goodbye, yes
to the first two people on earth who ever held hands and yes to
the touch of another, whoever he or she may be, yes to the long
kiss and short peck on the cheek and yes to the period at the end
of every sentence, yes to its simple and dignified mark of con-
clusion and finis, yes to the last page written in this book of flesh
turned on its back once more in an open field to gaze up at the
night sky of stars wheeling in the wake of so much dark silence.

Soul Ink

Deep down in this ink of morning I write because I must, I write
because the feelings overwhelm and the feelings inform in tender-
most leaning, I write with the toppling staircase of my life and
because the hours are short, the hours are burning with fever,
the tiny magnets inside my head keep leading me to rivers and
because here now is all I have, all I am given, writing the words
that come to me like precious wild animals out of the mists of the
rampant forest and writing the sounds that bespeak me, become
me, I keep writing with my dented forehead, my apoplectic fin-
gers, my palms whose lines are star-crossed lovers, CDs that skip
in the dark like Bruce Springsteen's *Nebraska*, write, write, writing
me oh, all my cherished beloveds and those who crawl on their
bellies, infirmities I write and rife afflictions, addictions, sand-
stones of great blocks of yearning and the lateral lines of fish gone
blind in the darkness of Lear's howling, still I write on alley walls,
on my own forearms in invisible ink, soul ink, I say, the calves
of former lovers in dreams who sleep beside me in small boats
of gentle cooing, on the spines of those who came before me
turning over gently in graves with eyes freshly woven into grass
and sockets cradling the stars, write, write, writing still because
today is here and fleeting and I have a plane and ocean to catch,
a whole sky, this page, this page, and how much I love thee and
black ink like blood that blots out (somehow) my many sins and
errors, the follies that had me reeling out of bars and bedrooms
piling up at the foot of my grave like broken wingless angels who

have somehow been given the permission to soar once more out of my creaking lungs, as so many clouds in the breathing of this world who made me and the trampled ground beneath and the roots of this earth teeming beyond this song, this howling, this plea of grace among the tumbling stones, a hundred ways to leave your lover and come home bleeding with scraped knees and elbows, heaven-bent on having the time of your life over this page, this wet, brimming ink, the blood that drips onto the hot dry stone writing our names in the overwhelming dark.

Water Is My Name

I feel a joy singing inside my blood no matter what I do or am, scarred and full of aches and remorse, hungover even, limping to the sink or the garden—and the joy keeps singing quietly, quietly ache upon ache and yearning evermore as when I was a boy and could not stop running in the woods and spokes of sunlight lighting the way threadbare and blinding roots of cause, the joy, the joy, oh the secret and mysterious joy manifest of branch and spirit and every mote of dust and miracle and tears washing over and grief though they do not soak or wash it away so the joy loves even my own tears and myriad mistakes, falls over them like limpid grace or is it only love and the joy, the joy finds me even now in gray middle age alone in a room just after dawn hearing the joy singing quietly to me, to everyone and everything, quiet, invisible joy who knows only somehow to praise without ceasing all the days of my life through fire and winter and the loss of the ones I love, this mysterious joy after and inside the dry ink of a comma, a period, the rings deep inside a swaying tree counting off the years of growth and listening and faithful endurance, the joy as quiet as the turning of a page in a library by someone who reads by the light of her own breathing and yearning for truth and beauty and surprise and the shock of recognition in a line of verse that this is who I am at the electric center of all there is, the joy of softly pressing down this one letter, one word at a time and a candle burning a few inches north of my elbow in great tender radiance, oh little star guiding me away from my many sins and sorrows, aureole of trembling brightness that must marry and make love to the joy deep inside me, rejoicing because I am here, here for now in the moment that is bud of flower and leaf, green and drinking sun and moon and drops of dew and every passing cloud and poem, oh the words rippling now like every river current I walk into, amazed that water is my name and my deliverance, the only answer to thirst and everlasting beauty that sweeps me forever away.

Other Darks

How to listen for a poem before dawn, how to touch the sacred night air and let it touch you, softly, softly, oh deep caress, how to wait for a word then a line then another, oh, over and over again, how to listen and how to wonder and the poem coming of itself, coming because it is wild and beautiful, coming because it is coming because it is coming and you know the deep shudder, the body not even its own but on loan from some mysterious creator who loves the body, loves even more the soul, this one and that one and how they are all truly one, my soul and your soul, dear hummingbird, dear 4:30 a.m. in the dark in the woods and these trembling fingers, how I am coming now, how I am henceforth and always your clumsy plaything, your ballerina, your deep sweet deepest night of pity and scrawled black ink, your racing poem in the dark and dear brother-sister poet writing somewhere in other darks, other kingdoms of loneliness and noun and verb (Who are we? Will this yearning ever end?) I reach out to you as we run to the sounds where we were born and my grandfathers' hands overtake the moons of my fingernails as I flare and flare and flare again, coming because I am broken, coming because I am ecstatic, coming so hard and fast and always I am salmon spawning my very last egg as my skin rots off my body until I am nothing but voice but, oh, for the clear seeing of these inner eyes, this paradise of deep listening, of crickets playing in the dark before dawn, before one page then another, poem I say and echo, poem as the last hope of this world, last tenderness, the last fey word or gesture and the whole earth a poem, a gasping, a lit candle in the dark flickering in the window before its dear precious lashes once more with fury and great ecstatic dancing and goes out, goes out, little wisp, little smoke, little figurine of longing rising briefly into the sighing summer air I know how to disappear, how to never be just this one body ever again.

O After O

To know you have been written on years ago by someone else's
hand, someone else's heart, to feel the words coming for me as
one of their forlorn own, to hear the ink deep inside me stir and
try to say, try to utter, oh, the most amazing and beautiful things,
O after O and then O again, the drop-dead center of nothing,
nowhere, nada, the gaping mouth I am heir to, this page and brief
racing of ink, my aging fingers, the joy deep inside my heart that
has no cause, no reason in this young century of mayhem, this
headlong sentence with humble radishes for company, dirt under
my fingernails and poems racing in my blood, to turn the pages
of a book written in Arabic, to know myself finally as one who
simply is with the earth beneath my feet, these rhapsodic words
that keep singing all praise to the sky and river and misty fog
hovering over the fields that is my one true breath and breathing
and every name whose shout and whisper is commensurate with
everything that runs and crawls and flies and stands, alacrity still
at the heart of every verb, every movement and stillness, every
longing and yearning stretched out to an eternal Y, the alphabet
I was born to play with, every back cast and false cast, every hook
embedded in my very own flesh, every stab of pain and clarity and
truth, every glass of vodka that tears Mary Ruefle's cellophane
cover off of this world, every poem I am given to write, memorize,
or recite not knowing what it means, only that it sings and hums
of a precious mystery and the clay that is this brief dancing body
whose limbs reach out to all there is, reaching for the oceans and

the mountains and windy plains, reaching even now, my love, to the ever-shimmering stars.

Note: The phrase "rip the cellophane off the world" is the last line in Mary Ruefle's poem "Tilapia."

Bell

I am a bell waiting for its chime, toll-bent in the middle of my life, just a bell whose roundness is assured forever (*wave* of gratitude), my copper folds waiting, echo of sighing heard long ago, heard listening now, waiting for a chime to claim me, pure tone, pure hum, pure moan (*wave* of wonder), and like a bell I hear heaven in a heartbeat, I hear tom-tom, tattoo of gladness, a dove in my hands who flew into the window and was struck perfect dead in all her parts and delicacy of feather, lineament of wing (*wave* of sorrow), and when I am struck like a bell I fill with the gladness and warmth of this aching voice, I get down on my knees and weep (*wave* of I-just-don't-know, *wave* of zenith center), and I lean into the holy flower of winter, I crystallize my breath in a poem in open-armed yearning, in gathering what petals I may (*wave* of astonishment, of being struck-alive these fifty years), and will bellwether, bellworthy my dry kneecaps cliff-face mirror of the divine rectitude and mercy and the patron saint of the misspelled word (*wave* of not-knowing, of the master class of kneeling), my bones a bell and my flesh a bell, my tongue a vibrating rhythm all its carpet own (*wave* of I-know-not-the-name-of-the-holiest-thing-so-I-will-call-it-love), chiming down the hallway of these given days, given unto me for now, for always, for the steelhead of my dreams I held in my hands once (*wave* of the wet teeming earth, *wave* of incarnate dripping rainbow that smelled of deepest woman), bell that walked this earth for now in galvanized rubber boots, bell that answers to the common name of Robert, bell that hordes and harbors pages of much loveliness, madness, letters written to the earth, the sky, the land of first kisses, the lonely boat of failure that caught and released a shimmering Niagara of fish, that stripped streamers until his fingers bled, that slipped down the rabbit hole of this sacred earth's dreaming of heaven dreaming of earth heaven, bell waiting for its struck wonder, bell on its clappered knees (*wave* of mystery, *wave* of the most imperfect electric slide), where, oh where is the perfect stroke to strike me, is it happening even now (*wave* of ecstasy, *wave* of your fey hand waving goodbye), who or what seizes this bell in holy sound, this sustained note on earth as it is in heaven so heaven is earth and earth is heaven as I ink and bleed down this page in human music (*wave* of pity, *wave* of grace), dripping out until the end.

To Beg Mercy of a Shadow

After Mandelstam

And to keep begging always in thumb-broken prayer, I a beggar and you a beggar of the soft luminescence and shadow, yes, the shadow of a pencil and the shadow of a book and how all darkness has its place in the widows of time, and how I am a shadow when I move between rooms and move between grief, when there is a whisper on my tongue and a whisper on my lips, when I don't have the words the shadow falls over me and I bow my head, and how would I want so dearly for one hour, one minute, one second for all the world's leaders to be beggars, to hold their hands together in one pleading fist for mercy, for light, for the shade of a shadow from the sun and their own wanton power, for the shadow of a missile or a bullet or the interrogation table, and how to beg mercy of a shadow, as Mandelstam wrote in a poem, how to walk in this valley of darkness and fear no evil, how to crack open this century with a sparkle of verse and love most scandalously all who persecute us, to beg mercy of a shadow, to beg mercy of a book, a poem, this scratching-out of lines like a mouse nibbling on a piece of cardboard, and how in such humble fervor the world is redeemed and almost saved and sanctified, how it is all coming down in the wind, I mean the titles and the fame and the factories, I mean the rape and violence committed upon this earth, how rapaciousness finally will go the way of all thunder and lightning into everlasting distance, how only poetry

and brook trout will save us from ourselves, how a single candle
flame says so quietly, Here is a bud of light in a sea of darkness,
Look over it and be faithful until the poem comes on the wings
of a breeze before flying away forever, before you breathe again
in the peaceful dark and whisper thank you, becoming one again
with the moon and the stars and all there is, even a chair missing
a leg in the corner, even a kiss on the forehead when you were a
child and almost innocent and almost worthy of the first streaking
brushstrokes of the eternal dawn.

I Who Wake Beside You

Do so quietly, reverently, as if for the very first time and it is the first time each time and always for what is left of this spent-most human flower, a crude and holy wilting and moaning of colors going down Moses as I hereby bequeath my last sighing and the echoes of ancestors, what is left of my body yours to harvest and to plant next to a cedar next to a river and purling ever after of a current and inside seam, bubble line and bird singing somewhere nearby, oh I who wake beside you not worthy of the smallest petal though there is a mote inside me, just a mote that might yet help light up the world or become an outstretched hand of offering, friendship, even love, I who wake beside you, I who stumble drunkenly down the home stretch for the umpteenth time, I who rant and weep, I who still believe in the crucified power of poetry to save the whole world, I who write with my entire body, every cell and DNA and saliva chart, may you learn ever after to forgive this foolishness, this headlong in the shadow of the long verb to be and we together form the pages of a poem called "This Window I Stare Out of Not Knowing What It Means" as an owl hoots in the dark and death draws nearer like a long drink of cool water or a mist over the fields before dawn holding its breath for all the world to gather into its lungs, to hold and cherish before breathing out again in the outstretched wings of a bird flying home to freedom.

Ordering a Book of Poems

And waiting for its deliverance, the slender leaf-bound kind thin as any sigh after lovemaking or planting a flower, frond of poem and page of poem and so much white space to wander and to wonder, oh book of poems on its way even now that I have never read, only heard as distant tone and echo coming closer, coming precious nearer, felt as keen inner ache and yearning and when you arrive a few days hence a part of me will also arrive, bird-beast and flower and vermiculation of wide-awake breathing and that will be a happy and hopeful day or maybe just the sliver of a bright, bright day and soft becoming, a shaft of brightness in this dark and noisy time, this time of rife extinctions and warmer temperatures, suicide bombers and domestic terrorists, but because I ordered you, oh book of poems, or rather begged you to come hither, I know beneath it all your quiet voice is talking and your quiet voice is singing, your quiet voice is whispering something beautiful, something mysterious and full of praise, even a shadow in a doorway and a peacock's feathers fanning out in glorious aureole, even the gloaming somewhere back in childhood when the face of God was reflected in a teaspoon at midnight or when someone you loved kissed a spiderweb or a cold pane of glass or when you thought for sure the wind was calling your name, asking you to come out into the dark night air and listen to the ancient echo of the stars and the history of every light, finding you in awe and rapt awakening at the beginning of the beginning of the beginning of your life that begins the second you hold the new book of poems in your hands and turn the very first page.

Dear Syllables

And the words take over, the words and their holy sounds making only the sense of flying birds, mating deer, endless hush of waving corn—and what the words, what the words and why and where are they going into what pages or corners and what arrangements, tattoos on the skin and the rusty sides of freight trains, the words spilling over, spilling forward, shameless, immodest words like buck naked, like wing-dinger and look, Ma, no hands, words sweet as honey and words hard as thumbtacks, thumbscrews and I let them tumble over me, tumble through me, word after word after word all the days of my life, as one son of earth and ancient pull of water deep down in the current where the one true ache is calling this turning world, the one making way for words like these, like page, book, fish, like early spring wind and the miraculous return of robins, like the rising sap still within me commensurate with the slow growth of trees, like all growth and greenness and how trees communicate with each other in holy silence and pheromone and the reaching-out of branches which is paradigm-shutter-map-most-hope of this world-giving outline of sky in glorious ache of feeling and how even now I know not what the words are telling me or where they are going but here we go again on our own, singeth White Snake, and if there is fire there is staring and there are poems yet to be spoken and written and I swear to you, dear syllables, I will do my utmost to become your worthy altar as willing sacrifice for your arrangement and utterance, the vast mercy or scream or whisper, the ink everywhere wet on my skin like the blood of an innocent animal baptizing me in a line of blazing verse.

Fish Me

When I wake I whisper rain, rain, as it falls and I feel as if it is happening to me slowly soaking the whole earth and rain, I whisper, rain come again good now, the good and simple rain, the mysterious rain that allows us to live on this precious besieged earth, cherish the rain and bless the rain as it blesses every one of us, every blade of grass, the rain falling in pellucid roundness and the Zion of the water bead, rain clearest ink of all writing poems of trees, flowers, and every greenness and every wound of light and rain writing with my lineament of hand and the rest of my body, which was conceived and birthed in rain, which dreams and sleeps in water every night, the rain touching rivers the most sacred caress and contact of all, rain on moving water adding water to itself, rain on a cold inside seam and rain staining the current and adding depth and layer and how many times I have waded in a river when it was raining and I felt myself turning back into water beneath my eyes and how rain in the air and water up to my hips I felt most connected and all primordial relationships humming a tender song in my veins which are themselves spring-fed streams with brook trout in every artery and I hope someone will fish my body one day as it rains and then there will be no inner and outer, no other, no stranger, like rain merging with a river by becoming river and my heart gladdening and lifting in this world of wet when even my tears fit into the mystery of it all and the earth is healed of our folly and our greed, with lightning in the distance showing us again and again how beautiful it all is, even if we are only able to see paradise in flashes that blind us, that fade away so shutter-still and quickly, that tumble us into church and hungry-most and thirsty desert seeing.

Let a Poem

Rain falling now speak my name and take me back to earliest utterance, first cry, first sound, let a poem rain over me, let it topple my spirit and my spine, what is a good water, rain speaking our names, everyone's, hush of droplets on the green, green leaves becoming me, let a poem wash over me, let it fill my veins to bursting, overflow, runoff, blown-out spring rivers, what is a good water, what is a current running down the middle of main street, what is the smoke and cinder of these pages turning into water again, these bones, the flashing vision of a fish in the first image of paradise, what is a good water and how would you pour it softly, softly over your lips and then down your throat, rain falling speaking our names, hymn and antiphon, the holy comma and clef note of a deer's track in the snow, what is a good water and what is a way to sing and moan it, oh what, what have we done, rain falling whispering our names or is it the secret names of trees, what is a good water, what is a good, good water and can you hold it in a clear glass, can it reflect sunlight and beads of dews, can it show you your whole life from cradle to coffin, every moment, every molecule, every tear and drop of sweat, rain falling now speak our every name and praise! Let a poem fill me with trembling and new curve of trembling, every roundness, every circle, every tombstone worn by wind and water, and what is, what is, dear Horatio, what is a good water and would we know/divine/discover/bow enough to recognize it, to ask for its forgiveness this day and the paradise all around us, rain falling now, teaching us color, teaching us thirst, teaching us how to take ink and use it in the liquid outpouring of our very souls, let a poem rush through me in fury and in praise and in the wildness of freedom to say what is already broken and shining, to move and fly as a bird over the ragged cliff-face of this wind-lashed page.

Plea

Only let it be love and let it rise in your chest like a sail out at sea filling with wind and sunlight above iridescent spray breaking into foam and let it be wild and ancient and let it sing in your throat swollen with praise and let it take up torch inside you, let it restore your dying sighs to grace and let the mourning dove find you awake before dawn with the smell of last night's rain reminding you of forever—only let it be love and laughter and let it be dancing on a gym floor, let it rock and wail and turn on a dime, only let it keep moving on its way to a stillness that is rapt and all-adoring, let it cook and clean with glee and let it romp in the dark-eating pages of verse and let it be poem, let it be deep delight, let it honey your mouth and let the leaves fall down in great windfall of color and let No turn into Yes and into another Yes, so many Yeses they can't be stopped or stayed, yes to love and whatever will be will be and on this day a wedding feast between your heart and the cornices of buildings and the upturned collars of strangers and let this wedding feast resound through the ages as a rollicking good time and a time to pop grapes into the beloved's mouth and let the consummation be instantaneous and impossible to stop and let your heart be open and encompassing of star and moon and nova, earthquake, speeding ticket and romper room, let us get on our knees and pray on street corners under the startled looks of crossing guards who will come to join us when they put down their stop signs and let this worshipping of is be our honeymoon only let it be love for it must be love and it is and it is and this can be proved by a coffee spoon and any quiet moment, a lit candle on a rickety table and the melted wax on its way to founding a cooling peninsula, let the envelopes sing with the slips inside them and let the junk mail grow into piles of glossiness and let the lyrical whatnot have its say here, there, and everywhere and always, even Wal*Mart and a strip mall outside Tucson, Arizona, the lyric of the doorstop and the lyric of the lightbulb and the lyric of the brick wall in the basement staring back that will yet give way to butterflies and parakeets and traffic soughing of motorists fleeing north to the woods and let it be affection, let it be a child's hand reaching for the swing on the first day of spring and this child's hand shaking with excitement, shaking from the chance to touch the sky and let the love wash over you and let it wash through you and let it be so grand and humble and tiny it can never be lost and let the love wear many masks and faces and none of them serious, let the love be daring in its foolishness, let the love tremble in its gentleness, let it brush away a hair from the beloved's face as if touching the hair of God and let the love look under couches and around corners, let it reach down even into sewers to see what it can touch and hold and let go of, let it be so full and deep no ocean could ever fathom it and let this love carry you to rivers where you may fall down and die to fame and let the love and only the love speak or say your name or any name, even aardvark, even Peter, Josh, and Sue, and let the naming be sweet on your tongue, something reverent, fuse box and window, gable and gimcrack, can that is kicked and can that is rusting from neglect and let this love and only this love lead you by the hand to a merry-go-round and all the painted ponies rising and falling in a circle that does not end, lapping again and again the great mysterious center as though they cannot believe their bountiful blessings and so seek to chase them down even as they are just out of reach above the unicorn's head that is another miracle without beginning and without end, so swing it.

Because of What My Brother Told Me

The ink runs wild and the salmon in my veins flash silvery and gold, heartbreaking colors and semaphore of most dire pressing irrepressible glad and because of what my brother said, what he spoke to me leaning into his tobacco-stained voice on the phone and because of the words he used, Lord, because of his gruff smoke-fueled voice, because his words traveled all the way from Chicago and Omaha long before, because of *Mutual of Omaha's Wild Kingdom*, because of the high blood pressure of giraffes and their long winding staircases of neck, because of ozone, contrails, a thousand holy miracles happening daily that you can't google, because I am poised over this piece of paper like an Acapulco cliff diver with his hands over his genitals, because I am in love with my wife and in love with my life, because what is given is not sown into the ground until it is paid for by one's dripping blood, because I would pick weeds on my hands and knees like my Hungarian grandmother, because I am river-haunted and bewitched by trout, wormholes and every vermiculation like a Sanskrit of mystic enigma, because of what my brother told me, because of the desperate love in his voice, because we fight and call each other bad names, because there is mud on my conscience and wild asparagus, because I am aging not gently but wilder than any buckaroo, because I am reading Belarusian poetry and burning with verse, with poem, going down in a heap of parentheses, because my brother said he loves me, because he said it once when we were both dying of excess and neglect, because I live to break new ground in the garden and to cast in a river seventy miles north of here, because of what is spoken and unspoken, because I tied a woolly bugger that sparkles like a diamond in the tiara of a beauty queen whose glacial gaze would kill you, because of what my brother told me half a century ago before we were born and parted our mother's thighs with great force and majesty, because we came out screaming and blind, ready at last for the world to grow and murder us, to show us the beauty of grass and water and the love of a good woman who would whisper to us when we had done all we had come here to do, the fire and the burning, the planting and the poem.

Any Word

Any word will do and I know that now, know it deep down and central in the great drip-drop of knowing, even Nazi if it's spelled backward to sound like *Ezan*, the Muslim call to prayer—and any word will do, shoe of wonder and shoe of plenty for today we will walk together hand-in-hand looking and listening for the bright scraps of words and leaves, oh any word will do, melting into this love, doorbell and footstep, any word the gentle but strong work of love, the word freedom and the new word raised here called lift-me-up-to-the-sky, compound of great felicity and fellow feeling the entire world over in electromagnetic force field, any word, any word, even bomb and missile, even assault and violence if they only turn toward the sun like radial flowers dropping their sharp dark hooks one by one until they glow, like roses sprouting from the open mouth of a cannon and then this great change and liberation of meaning, of dictionaries growing vines and leaves in word-plant kingdom called every brave and tender feeling, every river that shakes and trembles because it is alive, because it is beautiful, because it is life-giving even though it can drown you and sweep your body ever away, any word, any syllable, any letter and maybe O most of all, open and astonished O, O for God and O for lovemaking, O for the sound coming out of your mouth on the brink of blinding praise, and here these marks of black ink bear witness to the truth of is and the truth of noun and verb and the holy truth of a brook trout held briefly in one's wet hands before going back to river again, before the making of a poem which is a playful making and a gladness, a polished stone to stave off thirst, a new kind of hard gratitude that makes the world turn, a slope to race down circa the hills that are alive with the sound of music, a thrill of music deep, deeper, deepest in this human breast, trilling out a birdsong, a cricket's chirp, a woman's laughter in a garden with one of her sandals dangling and almost falling off her perfectly articulated and painted toes.

Bright Windowsill the Wondering

Always in this wondering I am, wondering how long it came to be this time and this place, the wondering, my fingers pressing down and uncertain with this pen on this page, fey wisp of for-ever almost, the wondering, wondering whether I will live out the day and wondering how far I have fallen and am falling still, the wondering, the vast teeming wondering and the wound in the wondering, the deep indecipherable wound, the wondering, the bright windowsill the wondering and can it / will it / must it be the wondering and can it save or redeem my wastrel life, the wondering, and will it / can it be wonderful, the wondering, and who must ask it and question the wondering not for answers per se, the wondering, and where will it lead, the wondering, the gaping ache the wondering, and how far will it take and plunge me, the wondering, and will I, can I go groping after answers, the wondering, can I, will I not finish the question, the wondering, the not knowing, the wondering with these empty hands and this shaking voice, the wondering, the endless not knowing, the wondering, and how quiet / still and prayerful of being, the wondering, here where I live, the wondering, where I cannot be but hurting, the wondering, and feeling all over, the wondering, and how it goes on and on and on, the wondering, take me to the mouth of a great sorrow and a great praise, the wondering, a great emptiness, a great howl down to the roots of a broken and forlorn tree, the wondering, waving all over as if to say and to sing, This world is my home and I will die here, waving my leaves and blossoms, waving a cosmic goodbye to earth and shadow and all there ever was, the wondering, ground, sky, and streaking star of an infinite goodbye twinkling, falling silver in your eyes.

Another Kind of Waking

And then the empty page again come morning, cloud unwritten on, virginal snow may I be worthy of your blissful stare slowly turning into smile, the tree that never harmed anyone until it was cut down and turned into this sheet of paper, a whole cloth becoming startled leaf of so much pressed yearning I can feel it all the way up into my eyeteeth, and here are a few feckless words to keep you company, a friendly tattoo down through the ages, a way to go sailing into the night darkness with a soft voice to accompany you, gentle passionate murmur which has been my whole life, I who have Emily Dickinsoned and Mandelstamed, I who have Jim Harrisoned and Paul Celaned, weaving once the leaves of another tree that gave me the single syllable O to run through every quaking morning, the O of my O of my dearest, lilting O not my own but on loan from on high, on high, peeling, threadbare O, every lovemaking shudder in the glissando spine God gave me to arch and to bend the arrow of desire in the bull's-eye center of desire's ground zero, O, I am epicenter of your awe and the ecstasy that embarrasses me until I am blushing bride turned buckaroo on the windswept plains of this earth, the ecstasy that sayeth you again and again and again that truly I am coming, Lord, I will deliver this letter and epistle, handwritten note that it is good and manifest of glory to wear this human coat of flesh, rock the Casbah, rock the tennis court and dance floor, cast to outside seam and bubble line where foam is home and home is a dog with a bone in his mouth, O, piece of paper, piece of paradise, how dearly do I know you here in the dark before dawn where I tremble like a leaf, piece of gently falling snow I catch on the carpet of my tongue to say/speak/whisper you now in all adoration, and how the pages of a book will turn themselves when no one is reading because the one who wrote them is turning them in dream spirit, in death, which is only another kind of dream, another kind of waking where the dream turns into birds and trees (the ones that were cut down, rising now in resurrection) and infinite light starring the pages until they burn and burnish and brightness with inconceivable meaning.

Dovelike

What if there were no answers but only questions, what if you woke one morning then another and another with only wonder, gratitude, what if the curtains billowed, yes, in the open window and cool mouth of breeze, what if you did not know, did not know, did not want to know—what if you went down with Moses on one knee in a garden of lilies and jasmine, what if the taste of a peach saved the soul of your taste buds, what if rapt and all adoring you became a wise child again, child of mercy and child of wonder, what if you saw beauty even in a tree stump, a murdered, severed tree whose trunk no longer grew into blossom and leaf like a bombed-out city, what if your hands floated dovelike above the page, what if your hands were beautiful instruments of grace and beauty both weaving in this broken world, caresses gone wild, holding so dearly then letting go like the last notes of a cello from a heartbreaking sonata, what if you waited for a book to be delivered and in the waiting you were somehow saved because you believed books could save your life and a book has saved your life, is saving you even now, books by Russian poets and books by Quakers, books so strange some kind of holy light shines up out of their pages, sunrise and gloaming and light not bound to any time of day but ether, ether, ether and starlight divine and page light so beautiful, so very, very beautiful, my darling, that you could not help but see there is an ocean of love all around you and you are swimming and drowning in it, my love, you are the dolphin and stingray and you are the wave that dissolves into holy mist and foam, the what-ifs taking you there, the what-ifs teaching you how to pray and how to love and how to laugh your own breathing in the dark when no one is home and you alone listen faithfully to the ever-weeping stars.

Essay Transparent Almost to Midnight

And so looking glass, looking through, essay the prose of almost clairvoyance, essay seeing what can't be said or spoken, essay seeing that the pumpkin seed and mountain are one, essay glowing like a low-wattage GE superhero, essay learning light in his bones down to marrow knowledge and the tunneling of rays, essay in a swarm from the first word to the last and essay as abandoned still as the wind-scrape of a child on a street corner in Detroit, essay taking the light and giving it back again in one utterance then another, then another, and one sentence for all in the clause of a heartbreaking mercy, essay clear as gin or a trout stream up north in the woods, essay clear running water and the trembling of water that knows no equal for clarity of life, clarity of love—and essay running water now almost to midnight, essay not hiding anything in obscure allusions or references, essay no learned doctor but naked savage, naked and clean-limbed beast leaping over a fire, essay quoting no one except the vapors of the dead that hang over the wetlands at dawn, essay misty-eyed and clothing the young deer with half-light and grayness, essay doing his noble work of simple declarative whatnot, essay in love with all infinitives especially to be, to be, essay a Romeo with a rose in mouth, essay on one knee asking a sycamore to marry him in bud-stoked union, essay fish-haunted and the flashing of scales before the fish goes out, goes down, vanishes in the whip finish of a boil, essay smooth as glass and see through again, essay wanting to be simple and pure and good while knowing his desires are a furnace cranking out heat and contrails but also the fervency of atavistic prayers, essay opaque, wormholed, dappled like a Petoskey stone when it comes to meaning, essay unable to fathom his own word-driven existence or the dream of rivers teeming in his veins, essay going, going, gone, now lighting out for the territory, for the hoof sparks of gleeful fleeing with the bit in his mouth and his wild eyes tearing it up for the warning track and beyond, essay galloping center fielder once more running down a line drive in the gap, I mean chasing the full moon down, the pill, the seed, catching it at full run at the end of his outstretched glove while the fans in the bleachers lose their voices, cheering on his reckless abandon and giving up his word-strewn body and the cheetah in his legs as they roar and cheer because he got the jump of a lifetime, a universe, one gleaming star with a singer belting out his song at the top of that cold shining world for now, for always, for forever.

The Woman in Me

The woman in me is writing this down—I was born of a single candle flame flickering before dawn—daddy was someone I loved/feared, I picked daisies, I was daisies, I am daisies. The woman in me is watchful and alive—I haven't held her hand for months. I'm afraid it will feel like molten lava—she wants to weep, she wants to laugh but not to shop—she reads a letter by a window Vermeered in stillness. She is my mother, my sister, a waitress—the woman in me is high on pastel colors, is wary of men in pickup trucks, low rumble of chassis then backfiring at a stoplight. The woman in me is writing madly in her diary that there's no proper outlet for hysterical laughter—she is running barefoot through a field. I never knew hair could smell so mossy. I didn't know my own fingernails reflected the almost full moon. The woman in me scares the shit out of me—she is the earth, every river I have ever waded or dreamed of. She is the fish I try to catch and the fish I do catch whose wormholes make me feel a world of holiness. I want to touch the woman in me—okay, I want to cradle her face in my hands—okay, I'm afraid to. I like how she sits hugging her bare knees with a the faint mustache of root beer on her upper lip—I like her strawberry-colored hair, then blonde, then dark, a few wisps over her left eye hiding a lifetime of secret hurt. Yes, the moon—yes, the oceans, the changing of the seasons. The woman in me, I have come to count on her, to make me feel things that tremble throughout my sensorium, that ripple out to the timorous stars—the woman in me is writing this. She is pen and ink—I take a shower and admire the beads of water running down her thighs. I am always bashful in front of her, can hardly meet her eyes. She says let it be, let it be, and when I look at her for too long I feel myself melting and going back to water, the man I once was running after her with flowers in his mouth falling away one by withering one.

Even If

Even if we drew nothing but flowers, spoke nothing but flowers, touched nothing but rose petals and leaves—even if we made love daily as a protest against injustice and murder, even if the very highways and roadside ditches were strewn with shreds of tattered poems and gullies overflowed with the runoff of unfulfilled hopes and dreams, even if, even if, my love, you turned your face to the sun in early May like a sunflower, a radial dish of much tenderness and beauty as if you were to ask the sun, the sky, the stars a childlike question and even if, even if we were to never stop running in a forest up north in the untamed woods, this secret, mysterious joy would somehow follow and overtake us, even if we go down stumbling, even if we break our bones, even if the government should try to stop us, try to silence us, try to police our very thoughts, the delicate flower of this joy would somehow fill us and suffuse our very veins, the joy of being, the joy of breathing, this joy, my love that recognizes no borders, no colors, no nations, here the joy and always the joy and constant the joy even in the midst of every persecution, indifference, cruelty, the stomping of military boots, the smoking and spent casings of bullets for all the joy that is the joy that will be the joy and one shining brook trout in my wet fingers for three seconds then gone back to tumbling water again, even if, even if and surmounting, even if and preposition without equal in the land of moan and groan and squeal of delight and protest, a coffin lid as a makeshift surface to draw and write a hymn and for simple repast of bread and water on the plane of death, the joy of a sprinkle of salt, the clinking of glasses over our newly dug graves, the joy or rich dark soil and our breaths while we still have them, helping the grass to grow and the flowers to blossom, tell me what is treelike and what is more magical than this, that we grow the earth with every word we utter, every sound, treelike ourselves.

Dithyramb

And then my bones began to dance inside my body all by themselves, my veins, my organs, flutter of eyelids made from my mother's own, all moving to some unheard melody deep inside me—or was it the earth, yes, it must have been, that time, this time—and I felt the inner dancing and inner rhythm as something beautiful and trembling god-most to a fingertip, a boy who could not tie his shoelaces fast enough (fast enough!) to go outside and play, a young bird in first flight for the very first time, the love of music heard and hummed in my blood in pure vibration, first kiss, first leap of a fawn and speckled trout caught on the first cast upstream, oh this inner dancing and the dancing of words on a page, a flower in perfect pellucid bloom, a woman's beautiful long legs, oh the first glass of vodka then another, poem from some unknown poet read for the first time (and how did he do that, how did she do that?), one cricket singing in summer under a full moon, the rustling of sheets of someone you love sleeping beside you, the first time I said, you said, I love you, I love you, a grain stack suffused with sunlight in a field with tender distance all around it dappling back dust motes of forever, this black ink on a piece of paper not knowing where it's going or what it means, all my holy and foolish mistakes, rain streaking down the window in January instead of snow, a prayer on the tip of my tongue pouring over into whispered praise, these bones of mine on loan from the earth and interstellar veils of sweeping dust, how I feel them aching to move again, how I feel them magnet-centered and pulled to a river up north, glistening and ever new after the first flashing second of astonishing and revelatory, incantatory, and miraculous first day of the world and open-mouthed resuscitation given over to awe-laden and gobsmacked dawn.

Essay as the World's Worst Jeweler

For he has been balled up and thrown away ten thousand times into the valley of the skull and scrap heaps only to pogo like a severed leafy head down the cobblestones of nil and so he loves and cherishes all flaws as he is profound flaw himself in his effort to be and to say and has been retrieved and flattened like a crinkled map whose coordinates point to pure wandering, no destination or x marking the spot but walking flaneur meditation on a button or a doorknob or one day last summer when essay fell asleep in a meadow and little birds entered his mouth one by one and essay is wary and even afraid of any perceived perfection or striving after thereto, essay digressing constantly and asking questions for which there are no answers—will you marry me, the bark of a cherrywood tree—and will you seek to enter the temple of a fish by way of artificial fly, outlandish streamer, the nymph named after a prince with the feathers of a peacock, and essay doesn't even believe in the value of pearls or gems but adores the least humble pebble and stone at the bottom of a river, where he often wanders and wades like a gobsmacked fool, essay on an errand of ecstasy and union with a floating leaf, a bald eagle feather or any precious and windblown thing that was once a part of flight, for essay dreams of flying and hopes his one-page self will be turned into a paper airplane by a child's loving hands with the aerodynamics of an arrow so that he may soar and coast as long as a breeze will take him, essay on the loose, essay gone wild, essay so briefly above the earth he can see and breathe almost all of it before he crashes into the ground or a hillside or even the haunches of a deer sipping from a stream at midnight below a harvest moon, for essay wishes to catalyze her startled leap in a graceful arc and parabola without equal in the annals of bound before Quick, look, there she goes and now she is gone dearer than any hush or murmur, heartbreaking ballet of vaulted alarm.

Maybe Fall to My Knees

What to do with this beauty, what to love of it—what almost
to sigh and to sing and even groan, what beauty, this beauty all
around, how every single day is sacred like drinking the very
air, and what to smack of it, what to wonder, what to dear Lord
truly you are manifest galore all around us, what to do with my
hands, your hands, embarrassment of palms and fingers and how
feeling greedy they are to touch and to hold and to grasp, oh I am
reaching out to you, beast and flower and holy breast, my hands
reaching out to the beautiful sun and the branches that hold so
much and so much lofting as the wind passes through them,
invisible clear lover and what to do, what to do, maybe fall to my
knees and thereby reenact the gratitude of the universe and rife
misspellings, on my knees to worship your navel slit-eyed and
most sacred and stretch marks, oh beautiful woman, what, what,
what to do with this inner and ongoing hum and faint vibra-
tion and condition of praise, how to feign normalcy—Very well,
thank you—and how do you do without Christopher Smarting
on every street corner even post–election 2016, what manifest
panorama and ring-a-ling-a-ding-dong crazy and madcap beauty
and Sophia Loren in every leaf and every bird, the sexual heat of
a doorknob and sometimes I think I will die screaming crazed for
the Beatles circa 1967 the year I was born not for Beatles per se
but I a single groupie of a poem then this poem then this poem,
oh I am truly crazed in my tweed pants and wool scarf as the first
frost descends in gentle forbearance and casements of ice, there is

no school, no curriculum, no Ten Commandments or *Bluebook*
to tell us its value or what to do with this beauty, this paradise all
around, and we're too busy to understand, too striving to ponder
the intricacy of a snowflake so I will do nothing, nothing, noting
with it but stand with Saint Francis in the garden and our dovelike
hands lifted to the sky and the beauty, the sheer over-awed beauty
of it all tearing us asunder and what a way to die, teeming us all
a beauty, and this the greatest destiny a person could ever have,
sing about, dig with a shovel, run around, dance, foam slightly at
the mouth, cast again and again in a cold, icy river as if his heart
is in every tight loop and it is and it is, hoping to catch the moon
or the stars or the lips of an angel to kiss me into smithereens.

I Write with the River

I write with the thorn of a flickering candle, I write with a grove of fireflies somewhere in Tuscany—and I write what can't be said or spoken, I write the impossible verb to be and to float, yes, even to fly, and when I write I am ancient falling-down ancestor who rises to his knees, then to his feet, yes, who wipes the sweat from his brow and continues the long journey with only the horizon to guide him and some inward song singing in his blood that comes out here and there as a moan and low force field of humming, faint vibration of Mmm, a sweet, aching sound full of the earth and human feeling, full of even forever, though he is already dying and the world writes me with my spine across the page and the chemicals of my body as ink and I take up torch of writing and I write with the lid of a garbage can, I write with a Native American drum made just for me, I write with torn sneakers and I write with a fly rod, oh bright precious loops of iridescent line, I write with my gums and knuckles, I write with the stubble of a three-day beard and I write with my kneecaps, Tina's long blonde hair, love poem after love poem, crazy nonsensical essay, I write with the river flowing all around me and through me also, under and over me, always, always, I dip my pen made of wind and earth into the cold clear current and I write that only this is true and brave, that this world of water may outlive us and become clean and pure again, I write how beautiful the poem will be when all people who ever lived or will live offer themselves to the beauty and salvation of this earth, this paradise, this superabundance of miracles as servants and singers of their praise planting a tree every day instead of pointing a gun or arguing this or that even as the whole world smolders all around us.

How Shall I Owl the Sound

How shall I say now now that I have been given how shall I
form and utter the words now how shall I begin whose very
thinness the whole world over how shall I owl the sound coo-
central coo-mystic owl deep in the night how shall I say now
that I am broken how shall I countenance the holy dark and do
it homage and heartbreak gentle song gentle overing Lorca's
wineglasses breaking at dawn how shall I but not I at all only
wonder, rippling like wind through the deep woods combing
their indescribable hair breathing this book of world for us that
shows us how to listen how to grieve and how to come out of the
forest as new men and women touched by beauty and touched
by wonder new instruments of a vast yet intimate strumming
in the violins of our souls orchestra pit of one and de profundis
as we wave upon wave take up music deep within and play our
solos for the crickets and field mice who play back for us and
how shall I holy gibberish how shall I break down in thunder
and sobbing how shall I sing this broken world back to healing
one lonely line at a time how shall I say I love you a new way
dew-touched and flower-most to a star how shall I this tiny
I this poem-crazed I hearing out our great mother's heartbeat
in the thick womb of time in seismic tremors electromagnetic
fields of pure vibration humming me now how shall the voice
come in what timbre in what key of tenderness in what soft-
ness of tongue and roof of mouth saying these words of holding
hands and feeling saying thy mercy and thy gentleness thy very
breath be spoken here on the altar of this page betoken me.

Bring the River

Bring the river to your lips and drink of it slowly, softly, the whole river and its mysteries and fishes and pebbles glistening in the shallows on a clear summer day, bring the river to your lips when you are sorrowful and when you are dying, when the world is turning to ash and smoke, and bring the river to your ears and bring the river to your eyes and let it wash over your listening and your seeing in keen knife blade flash of revelation, bring the river to your doorstep, bring the river to your deathbed and let it water these in great pouring tears, and bring the river to your dreams and wide-awake stillness, bring the river to your words and let them fall with spring water and rain and alluvial runoff and dripping leaves and bring the river wherever you go, whoever you are let the river restore your aching body to grace and bring the river to the playgrounds and to the schools and let the children run to it like little wild animals shrieking with joy and bring the river to the ticking of seconds and the hands of any clock, bring the river into churches and bring the river into prisons and let the river flow forth into this sentence, this phrase, river speech and turning verse and the slow accrual of algae and moss, bring the river, bring the river close to your heart and let it carry you to the mouth of a braver and sweeter utterance, oh, bring the river into the midst of all your fears and let the river take them and plunge them down into cold rushing clarity where they may dissolve and disappear and turn into foam of the river breathing for the greenness of this earth, for the greenness of this song, for the green, green power now greening in every life and every bird finding its own glorious way into the sky.

Pen

Your mind is a book; God is the pen.
MICHAEL BASSEY JOHNSON

And of all the pens in the world this black ink one suddenly most
precious, most central and most lovely, the one I hold in my hand
not my hand, any hand, any hand at all that holds this black ink
one gently pressed down into forever, how dear the black liquor
with which men and women write as Johnson once wrote, though
he did not include women which I include here now and always,
I exclude no one, not even the monster of my dreams, always
from black ink into vapor and utterance, I exclude no one from
the doorway of pen and I a pen myself writing almost nonsense,
gibberish, Motorola, my love, my dearest foremost self, I most
lascivious of verse and receiver of verse, poem is the dark and
light of myself, poem most high and down in the gutter where I
eat a raw radish like a shameless tart and how even now within
these words I can barely read them or make them out for poor,
poor penmanship that should shudder me into holy moaning
and prison cell though I am in deep, keening love with steelhead,
yes, I say it here, great fish, and ink, steelhead that are ink unto
themselves of great rivers and Lake Michigan, ink of the most
chromatic kind and metal head as I shiver here at this desk and
whisper river, river, river, ink of my blood as a quaking, wide-
awake fool who is faithful only to fish and poem and the fish that
are poems and I forsake all morality and grammar and tremble

only with a pen and a fly rod and once in a while a chalkboard, mighty slate, where I fail my students again and again and again though I am in love with their youth and beauty, I am in love with predawn poems, I am in love, yes, with Russian poetry and don't know how to rock it and page after page of glasnost, Siberia, Walt Whitman, hallelujah, who loves you baby, Celtic crosses, the overgrown mossy kind, and one frayed dictionary more thumbed upon, thumbed through more than any *Playboy*, as if I have been making love to the whole English language and I have and I have and I will and I am salmon struck, trout-blinded, spawn lover, instrument of crazy verse, official goner, lost seer of vast eternal grasses, here now then gone forever, wind-blasted root of a verb, bye-bye, hasta la vista, no one will ever love you more with three-day stubble and dance move, holy pivot, did you see the blue-winged olives in the cold, cold drizzle, I am going there, my hands a-tremble, holy smokes, one fish rising enough to save the whole world.

The Waft-Away World

And how it's floating away even now, ever lofting, ever praisewor-
thy and I waft with it in these words, spirit drifting, spirit soaring
and can we waft, you and I, can we seek the waft-away world
together arm in arm or dust motes of these human longings apart
and drifting, floating toward the ceiling or suspended mid-sigh
near the caverns of our open mouths and here is a featherweight
world and nothing to hold us down and gravity is defeated in
notes of song or a poem chanted from the depths of our innards
and waft-away world and disposable razors and recycled milk
cartons with the pictures of missing children stamped on their
sides in stark dot matrix deprived of wafting and taken away and
where is the wafting for them, where are the cries of lamentation
all the more precious dear, the waft-away world and scuttle of
leaves across the chiseled chin of a curb and all of my life, dear
Horatio, dear Martha and Saint Thérèse, I dreamed of wafting
and would wake in the middle of the night whispering "Waft
for me, waft for me," not knowing what I was saying or to whom
but waft, waft, waft for me, for all of us and show that it can be
done and that our souls are waft-worthy, the arches of our naked
feet leaping midstride over a watering can and to neighbors and
strangers I say, Waft with me, to terrorists and lumber barons,
CEOs of ruthless corporations waft with me, for the waft-away
world is revolutionary, epistolary, with letters flying and sashay-
ing through the air and hardly making a sound, give me a wand
and I will make wafting visible like a conductor standing over

an orchestra pit with my eyes closed as I wend and waft with my wand, with a swoon and a wobble as we make music together toward the waft-away world, O, my daughter never to be born called Wanda and where is Saint Wenceslaus and where is Willie Mays making a basket catch near the center-field wall then wheeling and throwing home and we wave and we cheer the staggering beauty and courage, running all of us for our lives after a fly ball, a drifting feather that dare not, dare not touch the ground in the waft-away world and the tears wet on our cheeks washing us as we raise our eyes to the Dog Star light-years away and the wafting constellations, the wafting words, the signature that is starlight and our inmost names.

Light Upon Lightly

To live lightly upon the earth as any leaf, feather, or rainbow, to leave almost nothing behind but a sigh, a whisper, a single poem entitled "Love *of* Brook Trout," to move while I am able, like a deer at the edge of a tree line, like a hare in winter over deep crystalline snow, all fur, all wide-eyed attention and in this attention the glory of the world, to forsake wealth and privilege and wear a belt made of frayed rope, to wear sandals fashioned out of old tire treads, to live so lightly my very eyelashes turn into commas between words of rapturous praise, to live so lightly I become / turn into light, the opening doorway kind, shaft of sunlight and rays of glory, so light upon lightly lighting the way for someone, anyone, even brother titmouse and sister sparrow, the cardinal who somehow appeared in a snowstorm in early March, a little bright dab of bleeding suffusing the whole continent, the whole world, bright singing bird whose beauty is manifest-ever-trust-ever-forever, whose cause and glory we will never understand, fathom, nor dissect in a textbook, perfect bird-color singing in ice and wind for no reason though maybe the whole earth is the reason and the power and the glory and the rain-soaked dream, maybe my own fingers scrawling these words, light upon lightly the holy cardinal now in recent memory saving me so vivid I swear she was an angel delivering a message of kingdom come, kingdom here now in the shocking present moment, her very redness a sacrament and a shining and the delicate lattice work of her bones, oh may it finally, verily come to us to make our own wings out of balsa wood, Styrofoam cups, anything light and airy and full of light like even, my love, this very page whose very ghost drifted down from a slain tree to sing and sigh of breeze again, north wind, this very breathing and dripping black ink, deep witness that fills the roots and pushes them to grow toward the one true light beckoning them with a whole body of brightness, a wound and a womb, primal throat of the first life and utterance, speaking for the first time.

A Kind of Inner Russia

But I wanted to say so much, a kind of holy rolling off the tongue up into the stars and darkness unimaginable whose ink drips like slugs of mercury from the eaves, and I wanted the words to move and fly in order to say beautiful, heartbreaking, and heartmaking things and have them echo back to me not in oracular outpouring per se but fellow feeling and fellow shout and whisper, this trailing echo and I somehow walking arm in arm down the streets of Samsun, Turkey, like I used to do with Kadir near the Black Sea and all those wind-roiled whitecaps unfurling their holy script back into the waves and I wanted the utterance to be all heart, heart of matter and heart of song and every living heart that wants so much to soar, I wanted the words to rise and fall in great tremolos of feeling and I wanted them to twirl on their axes like spinning tops or gyroscopes, spinning, spinning, overflowing with melody because they're alive and electric and I wanted to stoop down to the dirt and say Thank you, thank you, wanted to hold the friable earth in my hands and say Dear Brother, Dear Sister, destiny and clay out of which I was made and to which I will return release me now, and I wanted to hold this fistful of world and inhale its pungent vapors and I wanted to let it slip through my fingers in a wisp-laden goodbye as if it were I myself that was leaving, that was falling and it is and it was and it must be and I wanted to tell the people I love that the cogs of my mouth became locked in the Oh-dom of astonishing delight that could not end and not the Oh-dom of terror or fear, no, not the Oh-dom of regret, and

I wanted the words to be more than verbs and nouns, more than syllables scraping the roof of my mouth but palpable things like pebbles or stones or a single teardrop balanced on the tip of my tongue like a tiny jewel and I wanted the words to be like groans of sexual delight or outright cries of surprise, mewling sounds, purring sounds, rising and falling from peaks of gratitude and I wanted my voice to become polyphonic, metamorphic and multitudinous, a revved-up engine gunning for the highway as in a Springsteen song, like the waves of any sea or honking geese high in the air migrating to the magnetic poles and I wanted my voice to be stretched out and sustained like a cold bell struck perfectly in zero degree weather and frost casing my eyelashes, I wanted my voice to be a tree, a meadow, rain streaking across a windshield of a single mother's car on her way to work and I wanted my voice to be available for others if they so chose to use it and if they wanted to borrow a sound, a tone, a way of sighing for I have always felt this was the best thing I had to give, this voice, this sound and manner of speaking, which are not much but what I have to give on the altar that is body, and I thought of life as an ongoing process of developing this voice, of making it softer and making it louder and letting it trail off into silence, which is the greatest speech of all, and I wanted poem, I wanted starlight and I wanted somehow to express great distances both within and without and everywhere, a kind of inner Russia with its attendant railroad tracks trekking out across the tundra for thousands and thousands of miles, a post-Soviet longing of vast immensity and double-digit time zones for everything is written on and everything is uttered, everything is a word that had to be spoken or sung in order to be and everything is waiting to be named, and this inner Russia, this inner landscape of staggering beauty and unspoiled resources wants only to be sung or sighed, spoken or uttered so it can be praised and I give over to the whole sprawling book of it, its continental tome waiting to be set to music and therefore waiting to dance and laugh and pray so it can take its proper place among the mighty legends and the dear cherished listeners and pilgrims of song.

Because There Are Ghosts

Because there are ghosts in the cupboards and ghosts by the window, remembering old loves running ghost fingers through phantom hair, I'll try not to be nosey. Because ghosts float above my head and ghosts crawl through viaducts and sewers on their way back from hell, I'll try not to lose hope. Because the ghosts know me, because they listen so well, because they're tired of being blue, of walking through doorways without being noticed and slipping through keyholes on missions of great mercy, I'll wash my hands in the sink and try to do something good today, even if it's just planting some dill in the garden as I dream of future eggs. Because the ghosts stare at me and I can't see them, because I can only sense their presence as something fine and noble in the hushdom of a great silence made of precious air, because I sometimes think I was born in the wrong century and that I am John Keats's stillborn younger brother with a star in my mouth, because I remember the afterglow of tornadoes growing up in Nebraska and the otherworldly hues of chartreuse and sepia glaze on yonder blade of waving grass, because I am wishbone broken and part of an epoch intent on fratricide, because I like vodka and love the earth, because the ghosts bless me and everyone without a sound, watching me fall down on my cross-country skis as I struggle to get back up again, because I love a tiny woman whose laughter is lettuce-light like the rest of her, because I love Mahler and his bad heart and live in a town with the name of his unfaithful wife, because I play a drum in the morning and hear it in my chest all day long, because the ghosts are watching me, not intervening in the world of trouble and matter, because I will not stop for death though I know he'll stop for me, because a friend from Harlem described her dead mother with one eye open and the other closed with her lips parted in surprise as if dying was the most glorious thing she had ever seen, because the ghosts like the silent shimmer of leaf light and shadow on the late afternoon wall that have taken millions of years to get here, because I am ghost myself, because my dead grandfather gone for thirty years haunts me more dearly every day as I look into the same rivers he did, because Ghost #1 is communing with Ghost #2 and Mahler is a ghost composing in the Alps with the ghost of his daughter by his side with her ghost hand on his shoulder as he tries to keep from breaking down into a symphony of a hundred thousand dust motes—because ghost deer walk by our garden at midnight and I can hear them like shy dancers about to vault over the trees, because ghost word and ghost knuckle are strange bedfellows and ghost poem no longer wants to suffer and ghost violin plays ghost keys in ghost minor and ghost moon waits for ghost astronaut to wipe away his ghost footsteps with a ghost brush like a ghost umpire behind a see-through home plate—because Hamlet's father is a ghost and so is Shakespeare, who ghost wrote his plays with the Holy Ghost in mind and the native peoples of America revere the ghosts they call ancestors while most of us mock or dismiss them as hopelessly out of date, which is a crime that will be adjudicated in a ghost court and will render a terrible decision in the material world, because lust is ghost-shaped like a phallus and compassion is ghost-shaped like a kindly old woman leaning over an injured sparrow, because ghost is a noun is a verb is a sentence is a book is a hope is a love is a hurt is a woe is a shock is a thank-you card speckled with the blood of a pricked finger, because ghost is Chekhov's last train ticket punched before he coughed up his last blood, because ghost now, spirit now, all the ghosts crying, be kind to the world, be gentle, put away your guns, because ghost is the spider who watches me work and ghost is knowing that neither one of us knows what the other wants in ghost hiatus, ghost wonder, ghosting back now to songs of this heartbreaking earth.

Come Earthward

And now it's time to dance this very second no matter where you are or what ails you, even if you have shin splints, even if your feet are broken, and this can be proved with radiant clarity for the vast hegemony of cardiovascular reality, pumping heart, pumping blood and expanding and deflating lungs (can anyone fathom the miracle of this?), and what rhythms would you assume and what rhythms would you become, rhetorical questions pointing to the reality of verb and all holy movement and gesture, fey hand to the throat in feigned surprise, hand to the thigh for something deeper, something more pungent, a quick pivot of one's instep, the holy groin, a small leap over the puddle iridescent with motor oil, and would you dance with me, would you shake it and would that we become apples or stars in the motion of heavenly bodies come earthward, and we are and it is so and it's called this frail human vessel that's a tugboat of great dearness, hauling what it can in its wake, a few love letters, a battered suitcase filled with underwear that tend to fly out when tugboat takes a tight corner, labored breathing and a cough or two and would you Fred Astaire me, would you Ginger Rogers the sweeping staircase in glissando key C-major, for there is a wind that sweeps over all of us out of the valley of the dry bones that stare all day at the sun with their dry mouths hanging open, but we are still quick and lively and there are grooves in people, actual unplowed furrows deep as the night and it is glorious to move, glorious to walk and turn around and before the planet of arthritis and old age we were all swallows and leaping fawns—we were the world when it was young and there is stardust in us yet, so move while you still can, oh shake and wiggle it and use thy holy brow as lightning bolt for sweat and nodding yes, yes, yes to the two-step and boogie woogie you are a part of, the need to jump and slide and all the love you are heir to here in the kingdom of another given and totally gratuitous day.

Essay by the Black Sea

Makes way for other voices, other waves and ceaseless yearnings,
other seas and horizon all the way to Russia and essay out of
time moving through time and every molecule of memory, even
raindrop, even cursive of a crumpled love letter, full of wonder
and tea in a tulip-shaped glass filled to the rim and Rumi smil-
ing at all of us and essay that wants to try, that seeks to sing, to
touch, to hold, to understand, oh so gently in wandering, wonder-
wounded sense and the Hamlet of I, each word a velvet petal or
flower stooping to bless its words with colors, red or yellow, blue
or rainbow, and essay by the Black Sea not so black, but green,
green fading into emerald, into sky, into Russia and all the poetry
swinging in my blood, all the lost and crazy ones, my brothers,
my sisters, and Rumi my holy teacher, arm in arm and barefoot
on the page and so alive only a voice can say them in honeyed
song good for ache and word and love nest made of nectar and
cypress and trickling sand, toppled brick and mortar and waves
again like pages licked with foam and I an essay declaiming, I an
essay becoming the whatnot and the wantnot and the closer be
my beloved whimper and friend, Kadir again coming to help me
through my ignorance as I walk the streets of Samsun looking for
something, looking for flowers in headlong quest because Rumi
planted this seed in me, foremost errand of my spendthrift life—
and the Turkish girl telling me the story of her village where the
most important game is to see who can find the most flowers
walking down the mountain and then essay on the rocks and

stones and dusty footpaths down the mountain following her, essay in the sounds of sheep and sandals so worn their leather hearts can only take so much, crushed beneath again and again but somehow not defeated, not waylaid, craggy weeds and brush and essay walking down the side of a mountain in Turkey lagging behind, essay my heart following the girl to her village like a wild dog spent in wagging, and essay in her hands, essay in her fingertips, this love, this love, and prose overthrowing its bowers to run after and be inside her seeking flowers, essay my flower, essay my petal, this holy lilting, for I am prince of the apple core and sugar cube filling with tea and the flute separated from the reed bed lifting its notes high above the mountain, essaying this song to kingdom come and back again, blossoming.

Gobsmack Essay

I can't keep it in or keep it down, I mean the full-blown brunt of it and the hum and thrum and love of it and I mean the beauty, oh the drop-dead nectar of flower or shiny doorknob or lace of spiderweb lashing its way in the corner of a cold dark window as if to brush away a tear—and I'm unable, so, so unable to keep the doors and windows closed and the shirt on my back, the kiss on my lips from finding its bull's-eye pucker, the colors of any rainbow or any soft or numinous surface, and I can't keep it in and I won't keep it in for it keeps busting out all over and overflowing its banks, I mean the love, the joy, and the swing of it, I mean the heft and curly bangs and the hem trailing yon long robes of hereafter in the train of this now, this everywhere and nowhere, this once in a lifetime and this lifelong love of breath and song, for it must be sung or spoken, must be groaned or garbled, must be chock-full of praise for the windmill and the weather vane, the barn door and the shaft of sunlight coming into the hayloft in golden motes, and so this is an essay full of groaning, the ecstatic kind for today I found myself walking in the woods and whispering to all I saw (*groan with me*), the micro and the macro and little heart-shaped scuttling leaves, saying you are beautiful, little twig (*groan with me, please groan with me*), and you are beautiful, powerful oak, groaning even to the deer stand that you are beautiful also and the kill shot coming for all of us from a high-powered rifle a mile away, and I found myself growing straighter and straighter in my posture (*groan with me*) and hearing Black Elk's words to walk in a sacred manner and so I tried to walk in a sacred manner and I couldn't keep it in, the gaga and squeals of delight like Keith Jarrett at the keyboard and I couldn't keep it in and I didn't want to keep it in as even now in this repose I don't want to stifle it (*groan, groan, groan with me!*), no, not the nonsense of this praise nor the headlong wonder that drives it for it is not my own electricity but some mysterious voltage and I an imperfect conductor and then I understood or was given to know in blinding recognition like Paul knocked off his ass that I was never supposed to keep it in but let it out when I could (*so please, please groan with me*), that I'm not waterproof but water permeable, water soaked through and through to keep my body from burning up in ecstatic fever when it comes because I'm hot for the honey and couldn't stop the sudden surge that rippled through me, oh hot-wired bolts electric (*groan, groan, groan with me*), and I could tremble and quake without embarrassment in the land of the shining new verb that moved like an antelope leaping across the plains graceful in her parabolas and it was okay, okay, it was beautiful (*double g, double g, groan, groan, groan with me!*), beautiful even now to be unable to keep the beauty of the world at bay and to let it all in as if this body were just a sieve for holy rushing water and it is and it is and must be, cold rushing water immortal, cold rushing water please groan with me.

Ink of River

I look for ink like water, like starlight or the shadowy eaves of
alders on the bank of a river at midnight where I stand casting
my heart into the slow-sweeping current again and again, and I
look for ink bright as star and moonlight staring for every ghost
and pulling at the tides in the ancient song of wave, and I look
for deep dark ink to write me into a book of Psalms and hidden
scrolls out in a desert cave and ink to become me in headlong
sentence that writes itself in the dark with the words Oh and
God and honey, which come out of the same bright, blue center
that yearns and burns, and I look for ink to match the beauty of
a nightingale in pure-throated sound when ink is written in the
trill of poem taking dictation at the tribunal of roar, so ink me in
wild tattoo and ink the dwelling of early morning pause before
dawn to write and scratch with pen and this ink wild and incor-
ruptible, bursting like spray from an outboard cutting through
the lake and this ink like the blood coursing through every vein
and every other pent-up juice in great hydraulic pressure like
the force that through the green fuse drives the flower and every
greening power, *viriditas*, as Hildegard called it when she saw the
world as every blooming thing, and ink down in the earth where
the dead listen so carefully and faithfully, always leaning back to
listen ever better, their hair still growing and sending out feelers
for wind, bird, rain, and scuttled leaf, and ink broken yolk of sun
at dawn spilling over the land in pourable light to be drunk by
every thirsty flower and ink tumbler of vodka packing the punch

of moan, and ink tears distilled to pellucid, sacred water and *via dolorosa, via gaudium, delectatio, voluptas* and *paradisus* and ink of river where the fish are happy to lay their eggs and wait for spring, clear bright ink flowing across the skin of the world taking me home to mystery and wonder again, and every rise that seeks to fly all the way to spirit without end, amen.

Keeper Bees

And how they keep me, keep everyone, and with a taste of their honey I become the stars, I become the dawn and every particle of dust—I become birdsong and this heaving of heart, this song, this aliveness given over to making, to more song, more honey, all the love the world over, and I'm just a poet covered with bees for the bees have made me and keep me deep inside, honey, honey, and the love that persists and embraces all, even gutter mouse, even broken bottle and how all the debris conspires to make me whole out of every forlorn spirit and how my firstborn goldfinch shall be named Osip and how the Os shall sound for the rest of my life in dancing and grateful weeping, the full-blown and shaking kind that rocks the Greek Isles and churches made of stone, for I can tell the grandchildren I will never have that my weeping was pure in the valley of the turkey vultures and other ruminants and that I have loved who and what I did not understand and the hum of the highway called to me again and again and I walked toward it with my honey and cup of tea and how the Lord saved me in my vow of beauty so many times my knees became occasions for moss to grow on, and the almost infinite grass and how much I loved the ancient spirits guiding me, guiding me in my blindness and the bees who wove the honey I was carrying with their whole bodies and the sun, the sun, and I was heir to the kingdom of sweetness upon a morn and a taste of honey and how my tongue felt after tasting the honey again and again in order to contact grace and deliverance and let them travel down my throat and so it was okay to fall down and trip over myself for I was swallowing the sun and the stars knew my name in the book of intentions that continues to write itself in the miracle of the present moment and all of us restored and renewed, saved even, and assured for the rest of time as the clocks are vanquished and defeated and consigned to digital hell and all shall be well and every manner of thing shall be well as I used the honey as a salve on an open sore and it healed me as the highway spooled on and on, collecting voices, collecting tires, cherishing its broken glass from Michigan all the way to California and every small town in between that few have ever heard of, the billboards in catastrophic capital letters and the signs pointing west and even the state patrol aching for honey behind their shades and their holsters, empty of everything that matters as they track the speed of continental drivers with their radar guns, drivers who dream about honey even as they dream of love and freedom and want to live again as carefree and shrieking children in love with the drone of delirious bees.

Letter to Neruda

The moon of your skull is naked now and all your lovers have made themselves into birds and silk scarves and I think of you now at the beginning of September on a rainy day because you once asked in a poem, "Shepherd-boy, shepherd-boy, don't you know that they wait for you?" and it was like you were talking to me all the days of my life and the early morning hours before dawn where I wait for words to come in a room looking out on beanfields covered in mist and I wonder about you, Pablo, and dream that your fingers that once wrote out poems across a page like this one are buried now in dust and are dust themselves and I see flowers growing out of what is left of your mouth or maybe it is a star so you are able to rise above your poems because you are a poem and I am the shepherd boy left behind bereft of any sheep who remembers their baaing from a long time ago or was it a dream from another night, another morning when you spoke for me in a poem and asked me the question I could not answer that keeps asking itself in the dark with dearer and dearer insistence— "Shepherd-boy, shepherd-boy, don't you know that they wait for you?"—and even the small-town traffic lights of Alma ask this question, even the mist above the beanfields shredding themselves into the breathable earth—and it has taken all these years and many unfulfilled hopes to write you this letter for I too wait for my coming and want to die laughing though nothing is more surprising than to be alive right now and not know what I'm going to say or hear next, my own laughter, *sí*, or someone saying *buena suerte* to a stranger in the supermarket, and so please forgive this letter, Pablo, and its small freight of ignorance and not-knowing and the love of words that, who knows, may have already betrayed me a thousand times all the sweet and silent mornings in front of a lit candle that can be blown out any second which makes it more precious for its flickering apostrophe of light guiding me deeper into the heart of a great mystery, whispering sweet poem over and over again until it ends in a whimper.

Mother Forever

Nothing is wrong with this moment, and nothing isn't what I thought it was, which takes my breath away, not even what I thought was once important, which turned out not to be, and nothing is what I dream about when my dreams are clear and true like a house where everyone has moved away and the sunlight slowly sweeps into rooms as the shadows follow after them in playful but solemn fashion, so playful light, playful shadows, and nothing could be emptier, more damply, more open and encompassing of heart than this mother forever, and nothing is deeper than the winter silence right now this very moment, which is a tiny episodic prayer at the heart of all, winter stillness at the center of a greater stillness so also center of prayer, and nothing is not sacred, even windshield, even ice scraper and mailbox with its flag down like a dog's tongue after romping in the snow, and nothing is vaster than a chain-link fence and its pocket squares of chasm, of everlasting sky and the stars beyond, and nothing is dearer than this breath right now, my breath and every breath and your breath, dear listener, dear eavesdropper whoever you happen to be and whoever you are not, sweet god within, and nothing could be nobler than looking out a window, any window, nothing could be holier than to touch the cold cold glass with a fingertip raised as if to strike a piano key in E-minor, e-grateful, e-soulful, and nothing makes me gladder than the space heater by my feet glowing like a hot coal, like a little hell mouth, little furnace and little engine that could, and nothing is more beautiful than the cup of coffee next to my arm, warm bitter foot soldier in the war against nod, and nothing could be sweeter (once more) than this mother forever, this pint-sized little sweetheart and dewdrop, the span of these three seconds which scientists tell us is the span of the present moment but mother forever knows better, knows wiser, and she is sitting here with me with a smile on her face (though I can't see her I can feel the vibrations of her smile like tiny electromagnetic waves trembling across my skin), and nothing is preventing me from walking into paradise this very moment as I'm surprised and even shocked to find I'm beholden to nothing in the past, not even regret, not even remorse, and nothing stands in the way of my own smile, my own joy, which is even more surprising than watching the past rise up and fade away like tendrils of smoke and no one says I can't be Jesus, I can't be Mary, and no one says I can't be Rumi or a bird singing in a leafless tree because it can, because it must, because it wants to, because it was made for song because its song is praise because its song is love because its song travels the air to mother forever, to mother always who adores the bird and adores its singing and adores me, who cannot not adore and this all-adoring a kind of radiant shower that gives the rivers their flowing and the fishes their brilliant flashing of color and now mother forever is kissing me on the top of my head and I bow under her as we both say thank you though to what or to whom it's impossible to say but maybe is, maybe am, maybe here now this day this December, this basement, these hands, this breathing, this life and all life everywhere and everything, even a broken parking meter, even a concrete wall, even the spiderweb above my head canted in the gray winter light, waving gently to and fro because someone unseen, unspoken, and unknown blows on it gently in quietest play.

Play

Play now the dust that is day and play the leaves that scrape over the cold pavement in the play that is autumn—play the ink of dark at night and the morning that breaks into shining going down in glory again in truth of fading light, and play with the words you want to sing, and play with each other tenderly, oh beloved and friend, sweet confidant, sweet helpmate, play with your hands and your feet and play the deep musical chords struck within that want to be strummed, plucked and stroked, play the words you want to sing and play with a spoon in your fingers, lovely little fiddle made out of polished metal, play with the night again until it is dawn and play with the fact of dying, which in other annals is a stark reckoning of runaway doom, and play the sorrow that is dear for play is ocean and play is sky and play is the first kiss and the last kiss as long as we both shall live and play is fish rising for a fly in a brief boil of water and the heartbeat that goes boom and play is first frost in fractals of shattered light and play is moon watching out of cavernous stone that is a prayer of stone shaped by silence with pockmarks conferring a scarred but noble countenance that is no mere expression, and play is roof pointing to the stars and play is starlight gone out long ago and play is light reaching us from the past into now, into always, into what will befall us, sweet brother, sweet sister, play in water washing over sand castles made by a child's hands in most excellent, excellent play even when it is washed away, and play is basement window I look up out of each day, each playful, play-most day, and play is spider lowering itself down on a single filament of thread so silky and thin it can't be seen which is astonishing play of staggering beauty and play is root cellar, play is cauliflower, ruta-bagas, and doctrine of signatures where everything writes its holy name and play is the drama called living and breathing, moving and feeling so one must move, must play, must dance, must sing, must shout, must laugh, must cry, must play, and playing we make our beds and playing we mow the yard and playing I saw that I was a boy again trembling to tie his shoes to go outside and play with his friends and dear dying Ellen on her deathbed who kept saying, I just want to play, I just want to play, she who was all of seventy-five, and in summer I see butterflies playing among the flowers oh so delicately, and oh so reverently and the slow flutter of their wings that would grow so still before they flew away in great looping delirium, and playing were the hummingbirds and the rapid bruise of their tiny wings that bruised my own heart and made it ache and play I hear my wife laughing on the phone, a clean, beautiful laugh that somehow sends shock waves down all eternity where everything and everyone is playing, and play the farmer's almanac and play the traffic jams (see how all the headlights form a necklace like a drawn-out kiss and every car, every truck wanting to kiss but too shy to do so), and would the judgment come down on me with its fraught, implicit question, What did you do with your life, What did you do, I want to say, I want to answer, I played, I played, I spent my days playing and judge will then (I know it, I feel it all around me, inside me for I am everywhere and always, not just this body for the proof of it is the wind that will take my name away) come forward not in black robe but as flickering light that beckons getting brighter and brighter but never blinding, no, not ever, not that kind of

heat, only bright, bright, here, here, and then I will be taken into the light in first and last playing, alpha, omega, big dog and best friend in the frolic that does not end, like a kid jumping over a bucket or a fence, shrieking with joy as he does so.

Read to You

May I read to you tonight, may I pour out my voice to you, lowering the sluice gates, opening the windows of my mouth and birds bursting forth in so many words, and may I read to you, may I recite from the book of trembling vertebrae, may I offer you the least trickling grain of my voice, may I give you the dear moisture of my held breath in slow exhalation, the faint and groaning cry, and may I read to you and in the act be unrestrained, unhinged even, south of any control and a little wobbly at the knees, a little staggering, may I say tender and astonishing things, heart-most pumping blood and chlorophyll, the words a kind of chemical urgency, transfusion, transference, a holy cocktail, and may I read, read, read to you, Oh beloved and cherished listener, the one who takes the words into the delicate petals of your ears and the petals of your body, my body, our oneness in reading, our oneness in listening, and may I read not knowing what I'm saying in a delirious moan and not knowing where the words are coming from or even what they mean, strange country of wild utterance where the people dance like candle flames and weave baskets out of strips of bark and coconut husks, and may I read from the precarious edge of a great reverence and holy dread, the dread of my own voice, the dread speaking me now and writing me in the dark of myself where the words foment and turn over in whispering quakings of sound, wild animals and birds and visions of paradise, and may I read to you from the white hot molten center of a word in the glowing kingdom of a sentence, the flammable ink, the glycerin of verb, and if when I read may I also say thank you, thank you, thank you somewhere below the register of my voice whose headwaters originate at the base of my spine where the heavy lifting happens, Archimedes with any old place to stand and rusty lever leaning against the wall, and may I read to you, dear lover, dear friend, precious one who would hear me and want to listen when I don't even know what I'm saying, am reading and the tears in our eyes a holy fountain, beautiful pools, the words I read not my words but somehow mine to read and call out to you at the bottom of yourself and a bird watching over us during the reading ready to fly up at once in a flash of glorious wings when the last word is spoken and falls away into the vast and all-astonishing silence.

Somewhere a Siren

Somewhere a siren and somewhere a response out in darkest space resplendent with all nil, and somewhere a longing arcing deep into the night where someone wanders or lies alone, uncertain and unaided by religion or any moral comfort, a whistle unused on a table in a motel room though its shrill warning is never far from somebody's pursed lips. And somewhere another siren and still another and yourself lying in bed a stranger, a near outcast on the fringe of an urban galaxy, some kind of heartbroken freak, wondering in early a.m. darkness what to make of your life or any life, when you think you hear a siren sounding somewhere though maybe it's just the combined effect of ceiling fan and shifting isobars of barometric pressure, the branches of a tree lashing high above, but even if a siren is not sounding you know it has or will again or is even now somewhere else in another city close by or far away, the siren that will one day sound for you with no way to gainsay its howling arrival, and so mystical sound of an approaching end or terminus that can't be spoken or uttered, plinth of night and alone in narrow beds with sheets damp with fever, feeling that something is coming, some long-defrayed bill or reckoning, and is the body really such a poor shelter and such a rickety one brother ass, as Saint Francis called it, something to also pity, also forgive as it will sooner or later break down, and there's a siren for this also but an inward one called all my rushing blood and everyone's, coursing through whatever night on the edge of tender prayer and this same prayer one of ragged nobility even if it never makes a sound and the siren must know this somehow as does every emergency, and emergency a state of great alarum cry, an unforeseen occurrence requiring immediate attention as we emerge from one thing to another, chrysalis to butterfly, butterfly to angel, then back to eggshell or torn envelope, desiccated leaf about to blow away or up against a chain-link fence next to the runny ink of a wet newspaper or other scrap of litter, and somewhere a siren is growing louder then softer in a strung-out wail and when you hear it you'll know your whole life is audition and rapt attention, that not knowing what you hear and not understanding what it means is commensurate with a vast innocence washed clean of all presumption, the board we walk on and the echo we cry after and the siren knows this in shrill objectivity, swooping up and down sonic peaks and valleys in its relentless nocturnal enterprise encompassing everyone who hears it—and if I could say a few words to siren they would be Please lift me gently from the shelf of my body, and Can I, siren, laugh once more with the people I love, can I walk down the street with them arm in arm singing silly love songs and can I please, Oh siren, stand again in a rainstorm and stick out my tongue to receive the rain however it deigns to timpani my face and I will do my best to curb my greed for beauty so thank you siren, thank you 911 rushing through the night to get there before someone passes out or dies from blood loss, seizure, scalp wounds, cardiac arrest, and siren coming for me, coming for you, coming always, grant that I be gentle and faithful in my dying, that I wait in the dark like I'm waiting now for something to pass through me in a state not devoid of grace, and somewhere a siren already announces its formal edict and I hear it as the underpinnings of a mysterious truth rising and falling on waves riding the late-night air, for here is a way to be carried from this world to the next and it has something to do with Eustachian tube, cochlea, inner ear, and a concrete tunnel whose walls are wet from rain with flashing red lights rushing past the speed limit, siren sounding its headlong summons and lament, the emergency it was meant to broadcast out into the night to the injured and the dying, the ones waiting to be delivered from the cramped precincts of the body to a field waylaid by so much staggering sky.

Some Kind of Holiness

Then I didn't go back, and I never returned. And I was never the same, not even the way I looked at sunlight lofting through the tree or heard birds singing of the seasons and their own hymns of flying. And I told the air, I told the earth, I told the sky I couldn't do it anymore, and oh how they understood, oh how they cherished the surrender and the awakening that was like coming to water for the first time—and then I started to look for materials to build my own wings and flight became a living, wide-awake dream bent on destiny and it was not far-fetched, not impossible, but something just out of reach that I was getting ever closer to and then I saw the earth as an acorn in a little girl's hand proffered shyly for my consideration, and then I was delight, I was laughter, I was sexual surprise, I was streaming, I was sunshine, I was rain, I was treetop, I was color-bursting flower and petals floppy and wet with dew, and I was another bird singing and another bird racing through the air with wings flashing like rainbow, and then I couldn't not whisper paradise, I couldn't not say lovely and uppermost, couldn't not say beautiful fish, and I didn't go back and I wouldn't go back because the holiness had claimed me, even if they tried to drag me back, and then I could breathe and I knew I would never return, that I would never go back to that place, and then I could no longer taste bitterness though I could taste sorrow, and then I went to the heart of nectar in a warm chemical bath and I said Rise to the river and the river rose as if to wash over me and then all around was a shining light that almost burned off my eyebrows, and then I was grape, I was wine, and then the waving grass sang to me and I opened my hands and they were wet with tears and then I felt seizures of electricity deep within and I knew weather was ancient and wise and always, and then I asked to take the torch and knew myself as fire, as immolation and sacrifice, as some kind of holiness, talisman of blessing and choir of many moons and many summers, and then a stranger took my hand and kissed it, and then I got down on my knees at the mouth of a river, and then I stroked the fur of the wild dog who suddenly appeared before me and his fur gave off blue sparks and magic, and then I tried to howl at the stars and then the voice of God spoke to me and said Be patient, Be gentle, and then I read the poems deep inside the grooves of bark and then I started sucking on a pebble to stave off desert thirst and the madcap speeches starting to claim me in gusts of headlong praise and then a single falling leaf held me in rapt beholding and a great light broke over my head in halo, and then I memorized the prayer that does not end and always begin with Dear Creator Spirit and then I was notebook spiraling out of control and I knew raiment, I knew the secrets of color and I couldn't go back anymore to that other place wracked with doubt and fear though traces of it remained in the smell of burnt rubber and then freedom crowned me with a sycamore branch and all I could say was Star, star, beautiful star, and then I reached out to you, I reached out to everyone, and then I said Love and I said Poem and I said Forgive me and I said Unspeakable beauty and then I said Thy will be done and I said My, what a beautiful cake and I said Thou movest me and I said Let's dance on the bar and I said I'm hard from all this wanting and I said I once held a fish and it was like holding the whole world and I was, I was, and I said Take my hand and I said Take my arm and then I knew what heaven was, what it really is, and I knew I didn't have to be afraid of men with guns and official stamps and then I knew I was almost free, that I was almost ready for nuptials, that my life, any life was an astonishing occurrence that would not end but morph into a different set of colors, and then I said as clearly and evenly as it was in me to speak, I can't go back and I won't go back and this is the writ and the proof of it, for even my blood has changed back to the shining ink of stars: and so Father, Mother, Brother, Sister and all the dearly departed, you don't have to hold the door for me. See, I have already sailed right on through like a sudden breeze, light as breathing after much labor and struggle in the rest that comes at end of day and the glass of red wine standing on the table as if it wants to whisper something very holy and very private and very, very simple, something like peace.

When Water This Earth

When water comes to me, when it appears in my dreams or in my waking, when I hear it running in a stream, a river, my inner ear, trailing molecules of mist—when water my love, my ageless, my drowning, when water, oh clarity, oh surrender, when it washes me in words, in birdsong, in poem and verse, when water says my name or births my name, when water becometh me in the dark before dawn where I wait for water words, when water this black ink and water my soul, my every love, when any animal bends to drink you, when animal bows down as if to pray for drinking you is a prayer, prayer of this earth, this clarity, this thirst and quenching of thirst, slake-driven and sucking on a pebble or a moss-covered stone, when I say water, two syllables, two beatitudes, when water taketh me over and water rolls over me, when it beads on my very skin, when it is wipered away on the windshield, when it slips through my fingers, when I know that the water hour is here and it is here, it is always, when water my fish, my singing line, when water collecteth me in tranquility and pellucid grace, when water stirreth me to action, to deep caress, to holy kiss, when I stand in the current hip-most to heaven and all the listening trees, when water this earth, this world, this one lightning and flash of shazam, when water pours me over again and again into praise, when water becomes ice, when water becomes cloud and fog and haloed molecule, when water carries me away to the mouth of a simple utterance, when I hold your hands in the water, when water rushes over and around all obstacles, all manmade foolishness and speed traps, when water floods this page, this heart, this wonder-wounded hearer, when water the Hamlet of I jumps into the grave, when water drips from my eyes, when water saves me, saves everyone, when water is born with the first breath and the last, when these words grow gills and slats for almost flying, when water tells me it's time to boogie, time to come home, oh I am going there, the holy ripple, the clear seam deep down in the mercy of its cold rushing, looking at me so deeply as if perchance to wash through every dryness, every last and overturned stone.

Tell Me Flower

And may the earth shine through your voice when you tell it in slanting rays of sunlight for there's an urgency inside us called flower and a frailty that tugs gently at the purse strings of death and if you make up a word for flower please do so only out of keening necessity and let your naming be a holy utterance and a way to love again, a way to become sky who is not just mother and father but also child wandering toward the horizon, and my word for flower is myriad, many words and many voices and gestures including hands folded in prayer, and flowering the dawn and flowering long past midnight where I lie listening for a flower to carry me away, hearing trains lamenting their separation from the common book of prayer, and when you tell me flower we will set out to gather raiment in sacred enterprise and hearing flower in each other's voices we will be renewed because all of earth is a garden waiting to be realized, which must be seen with eyes of sedum before it can become manifest and flowering, all seekers and believers and those who have lost their way, so tell me flower again and again as long as we both shall live and I will do the same in the litany of a sigh whose dominion has no opposite, and when you go to someone's house for dinner you take them flowers, and when someone dies you drop flowers into their graves and they fall like leaves or paper, and when you tell someone you love them you give them flowers, and when you are a woman you put flowers in your hair and flower is ready to explode in all directions, all occasions, a trip to the dentist, the tying of one's shoes, dropping change into a parking meter, so tell me flower, tell me rainbow, tell me radical new soil, for verily I dreamed of a flower or it dreamed of me and I saw flower everywhere, in chemical transference composting out of trash heap, broken refrigerators as limp resurrections, old dreams and sorrows, failure to post bail and the last time you were ridiculed or forsaken, forgotten, abandoned to die alone in a room not of your own choosing, and flower told me in shattered windows, abandoned buildings, the cracks of sidewalks wanting to be light again, the ghostly reflections off the hoods of cars and sunglasses donned by hit men, and when I was in extremis I said flower, whispered flower without letup or surcease to take beauty into darkness and thereby reclaim life-giving color and I could walk down the aisles of supermarkets and other megastores and say flower-full, flower-most, softly then louder then softly again so as not to be confused with Christopher Smart giddiness, and I approached everyone I saw like a beggar on a busy street, pleading with them to tell me flower, to speak its petaled name in miraculous gamma rays called shudder, called shiver of deliverance, for I yearn to know how to feed on light directly, not via esophagus and incisors and digestive tract, flower filtering me through a sieve of great tenderness as I could see with great rhapsodic clarity how to live and thrive even inside the creosote blotter of railroad tracks and all their clacking comeuppance, and 2013 tell me, speak me flower and 1812, pray me flower for what is needed now is needed always in streaming glossolalia and moon is a flower and ocean is a flower and together they make love and pen is a flower and glass is a flower and together they make love and fingernails flowering on the chalkboards of empty classrooms to scrape up meager praise and anthills flowering near the leaky skulls of the dead whose mouths are stuffed with cotton balls and flower the year of the tiger and year of the dragon, the hare racing for his hole with his ears pinned back for flying, flower may your voice be when it is time to sing, which is always now, and flower the woman's blue dress in Florence outside the train station where I left my dust in awe, flower, flower, flower and fleur-de-lis and the saints come marching in, fire is a flower and its flame is a tulip where I drink tea and flower is a poem, is a touch and caress and flower is a home where the seasons take root to kill us and give birth to us every winter and every spring and sunrise is a flower and so is the first bird singing before dawn up north in the woods next to the crumbling yellow shed that holds the wheelbarrow and the spade, the waders once filled with river water and all the tools to cultivate the holy soil, hoe, shovel, and watering can inside of which sits a toad and a cricket, quietly telling each other their dreams of flower, flowering themselves between a spiderweb and spokes of sunlight drilling their blossoms through the broken screen above.

The Most Woke

God of morning, how do you find me here again amazed with open hands and not-knowing, sister of morning whose dress is swept aside like ancient starlight, like the first touch of dawn in light that touches every fin and leaf, every branch and blossom, the most woke, the most awakened, a girl's kneecaps like skulls of glorious praise, god of morning and god of becoming, or are you just simple awakening in a new century where men murder trees and fields and the air with their greed and ignorance, or will you glory of morning overcome even these with the most woke and most betoken, your forever coming back and plinth of resurrection where I mote of sunlight do also rise once more to wonder and to wander down the hallway of my remaining days, whose waking dreams are filled with the iridescent colors of flashing fish and the river tugging around my knees and water so cold and clear it's how I see all the way to eternity, the most woke, the most delivereth of all, to the purity that speaks directly to the heartbeat of this earth and every living creature, even this sentence where I seek to live beyond any parenthesis or comma, line or boundary, the most woke, goddess of morning and fey lover and her warm naked thigh brushing against my own after dew of gentle waking and every tree outside rapt and attendant to thy just-born and glorious rising slowly above the curved shelf of this miraculous and thrumming world, the most woke, the most loving, and light again reflecting off a leaf, your face, these shining words, waking us to the only truth and beauty that ever was or shall be.

So Wild Beloved

So it came to me like the dusk and the dawn and the downpour, so wild beloved I could not keep up with myself or gainsay its arrival, too much of not enough and not enough always rampant in my breast, this wild beloved so eternally the vibrant always animal now and this same body that has been so faithful, so willing to walk through the woods and cast after cast after wording, so wild beloved, so completely humble and noteworthy, brother ass so willing to carry anything, firewood, dictionaries, vodka bottles, and piles of ash, so wild beloved, so breathing and true, pages like these strewn out like rife spent lovers of the most depleted kind, empty of themselves and all bodily fluids, my lips rampant to kiss any surface, any mouth, refrigerator door, graphite fly rod and enamel coffee cup Formica forever, so wild beloved methinks this page is spontaneously combusting into love letter, holy writ and scroll and holy gibberish, deep moan of prayer and thank-you, of hastily well met and every union card redeemed by mystical connection until we all are one, so wild beloved and The Complete Guide to Gardening published circa the pubis of any man, woman, or child who are flowers unto themselves, singing a cappella, slapping the rat in the middle of the night, which is a kind of radical free-fall fishing called mousing, called hide-and-seek and freshwater sharks, so wild beloved and every vermiculation and wormhole and rainstorm and so it came to me like the dust and the drapes and the dropper and the high-stepping dandies and the dandelions and the diphthongs and the dirigibles and the dominoes and dopplers and the D-major Hungarian folk dances that so wild beloved is here among us after all and we can lean into her, into him, and that all love is one and oneness, that like Edith we are a part of infinity even if we cough up blood and know not the true way north, it will still catch us and guide us, just wait human compass with metal filings in my head so I turn even now in the direction of my ancestors and almost fading voice, a whisper, a song, the gentle soughing of wings and now I am gone.

Note: The phrase "we are a part of infinity" comes from Edith Södergran's poem "The Triumph of Existing."

Gaze of a Child

Can you meet the gaze of a child, can you wander over it into purest seeing, can you meet the gaze of a child and would you then see lakes of eternity in her eyes, his eyes, can you, will you, would you meet the gaze of a child and go down Moses and Mary and all the saints, all the Godsmacked ones, will you touch the petals of a flower and thereby enact the miracle of tenderness where talus and cliff-face reign, can you meet the gaze of a child or will she will he tremble for all you have and have not done, the child watching you, staring at you, as does the whole blank universe of silence, whose stars are watchers as so many points of light that yet hold and cherish your every breath, your every waking, did you meet the gaze of a child when beauty first touched you, first held your hand in the valley of the most holy salvage, the renegade verb and the wild, wild words who have been stalking you all your life, was the child there, was the child also coming for or waiting in the middle of a field, was the child perfect with not knowing, with hearing the wind as foremost teacher and oracle and all the wild animals and the wind sighing of what is everlasting and true in this beautiful world, was the child is the child can the child be again in the midst of every joy and sorrow, every holding of flower, can you meet the gaze, the stare, the open eyes of the child, those worlds upon worlds upon plunging, can you meet the gaze of a child down by a river by a stream by a hollow with birds singing where you cannot see only hear them somehow in the child's eyes, who watch not to see what you do but who you are past the deer's bounding and the swooping of an owl's wings deep in the forest and mercy of sunlight stippling through the trees.

All I Feel Is Rivers

And dawn seeping over them, then slowly brighter and brighter until I am lit up by a cathedral of dust motes in the woods by another river and sheer majesty in my veins and hosanna praise my only voice. And all I feel is rivers, and all I ever wanted in clear rushing river speech which is my truest name and new rhythms and harmonies blessed by the earth and rain that blesses every branch, every leaf, my face, my eyes, my ever-newborn seeing that goes on almost forever, all I feel is rivers and the current is my life force, the current writes the poem and opens the flower, the current kisses the cold foreheads of the dead and the current makes love with the entire earth, the current walks the many miles and the current stacks the wood, weeds the garden—for all I ever feel is rivers, all I ever dreamed of becoming, the only emotion is water and it is rising up inside of me, all the rivers are converging in my heart and every fish, heron, and kingfisher, the rivers do me make and do me break, the rivers vision of paradise and all mother life in this world, holy breast and all fecundity, the birth canal of every verb, and all I feel is rivers, all I do not know and dream of is rivers in the sprawling ink and handwriting of the fields and mountains, the rivers leading me to books and far away, the rivers writing down the poems in the middle of the night and the rivers reciting them quietly like a bare hush of wind, rivers in my sweat and river in my gonads, the rivers as vast and teeming as the clouds, the stars, the river-born sentences as I take up their headwaters and all their outpourings, runoffs,

I a human river, a water poem, and water pouring through your fingers, your mouth, human oxbow of the holy bend and with a pebble and a snail as brother and sister, scribes who draw letters with their whole bodies all their lives, writing into that bed of stone words that will keep washing away forever.

God-Husks

I woke from a dream and nothing to write with, not even a gnawed-on pencil or nub of charcoal, God-husks all around me, God-husks as fallen bodies and spent mollusks, broken and used-up bodies, as I whispered God-husks, God-husks, and the room smelling of recent and sleep-pellucid rain. So I said, so I whispered, so I trembled, God-husks, only God-husks, and I was one of them, one of the fallen and discarded ones, a God-husk myself—and what did it feel like to know myself as a scrap heap diviner and pale afterglow, a God-husk feeling all over for some small crumb of the glowing eternity left for him to sup on, to drink through cracked lips and broken cistern, broken flower and all the lilting ones as another God-husk, and still another taught me how to crawl my way to imperfect and implausible praise, oh the God-husks flat everywhere and I took their fading glory into myself and wrote with my whole body and traces of DNA—I wrote with my saliva and sweat on the mirrored page and I wrote on the walls and windows and my very own skin as we are invited to do by all our flying brothers and sisters, finches, warblers, and the steadfast robins, God-husks themselves with feathers of the one true wings and flight over the burning fields and cities but also the clear rushing water of streams and rivers who know only gladness and such clear seeing maybe we are heir to after all and the God-husks of glowing pebbles and stones at the bottom of the river as the cleanest things on earth polished by almost endless seeing revealing the only way out, which is down, down, and down-most, surrendering our God-husks to the mighty current that seeks to sweep us ever away.

Becoming Less So

An ever-falling-in-love mystery, a sudden or gradual coming to, *Aha!* of the sweetest order, an empty bank account, empty tank of gas, a vast loosening of understanding or control, an explosion of birdsong in our chests, an ever-falling-in-love mystery and zero-sum game, a phi slamma jamma of high fives and most unworthy houseguest, who knows, no one knows what will happen next and whose knuckles will win the lottery of a kiss, what quaking body sobs will shudder thee in grief or ecstasy or grief in ecstasy, ecstasy in grief, how vast and beautiful the kingdom of not-knowing and not-needing-to-know, how fish-haunted and driven to almost river madness, wading to the end of my days and then somehow wading some more, only some heartbreaking, heartmending falling-in-love mystery the ink of this pen is fountainless or just forever pouring, forever bleeding what can't be said or uttered, groaned maybe or sighed like a few passing clouds high above, almost fifty-two now sitting over a blank piece of paper wondering what sound or phrase will say itself with feeling, desperate, sacred scratching of the oddest kind, kin to sea rhythms and leaf music and the scolding of redwing blackbirds, a little girl waving goodbye or a grown man confessing defeat on his knees with a little love song thrown in and a few streaks of rapture coming from who knows where, who knows why.